Perfect Dream

A Maverick Immigrant Boy's Journey from an Isolated Village to the American Dream

DR. KAMAL BEWAR

Edited by Jason Roberts

ISBN 979-8-88943-627-0 (paperback)
ISBN 979-8-88943-628-7 (digital)

Christian Faith Publishing
832 Park Avenue
Meadville, PA 16335
www.christianfaithpublishing.com

Printed in the United States of America

To my family, especially my dad, who taught me everything in life without any formal education

Contents

Prologue

I lay on my back in the warm bed, underneath an actual blanket. There was no artillery shelling outside, no air raid sirens, no shouting guards, no night patrol walking. The wind could not creep under the flap of a tent or through the threadbare sleeping bag. My belly was full from a hearty warm meal that wasn't just old beans or whatever could be scrounged from the countryside. There were no creatures crawling around in the dark, waiting to bite or sting. There were no troops somewhere in the dark that could attack at any minute. I didn't have my AK-47, and I didn't need one. The thick layer of dirt and grime was scraped off my body and washed down a drain with hot, clean water. There would be no night duty, no midnight foraging, and the future stretched in front of me as an open road of possibilities instead of empty dead ends. For the first time in nearly ten years, I was completely safe and full of hope. I fell asleep with a broad smile on my face and hadn't slept that well since the innocence of my childhood.

Introduction

I was born in Kurdistan, Iraq. I moved to the United States when I was twenty-three years old. Currently, I am working as a Student Success coordinator with the Salt Lake Community College at the Office of Diversity and Multicultural Affairs. Recently, after many years, I completed my doctoral degree, in higher educational leadership.

Just after completing my doctoral degree, I realized the needs of my Kurdish community in Utah, and I decided to spend and deduct more time serving my people to the best ability. I have worked along with some of my Kurdish community members to establish a non-profit organization under the name Kurdish Community of Utah. The purpose of this organization is to create a family-friendly atmosphere for all Kurdish families here in Utah, in addition to introducing Kurdish culture to the communities in Utah. After forming the community, we have been able to participate in many different events, such as Annual Refugee Day and Local Community Event Night.

Also, I have offered to teach Kurdish to our Kurdish children during the weekends to ensure Kurdish children know their mother tongue and their culture. For me, it is important for each of us to know who we are and where we have come from. I believe we should all know our backgrounds; it helps us to identify ourselves here, knowing where we originally came from.

The purpose of this memoir is to let others know some of the events of my life and how important it is to keep fighting for what you believe in. More especially, I want to let my beloved son read my memoir, perhaps when he's older, to understand and appreciate the kind of life that he has been given. In addition, I want to ensure that my readers see how other people live and immigrants who are seeking a better life have endured unbelievable hardship. I hope they learn something from this valuable memoir and understand that in life, nothing is easy or impossible.

Occasionally, I reflect and think about my life. It gives me a sense of pride in what I have accomplished as an immigrant in this great country, where I started in the last twenty-six years, the difficulties I have had all these years and at the same time still moving forward to the next chapter of my life. Furthermore, when I think about my sense of pride occasionally, I feel embarrassed at the same time. Like any other human being, I could have done things differently, or I could have made better decisions. Nevertheless, as a human being, no one is perfect! Someone only can hope for an opportunity to think about a lesson learned. Here I am in my late forties, still learning lessons to enhance my ability to ensure as a person to become a productive individual in our society. Each day, I learn something new, and I realize life is a school of opportunity. In order to take you to the next stage, I have to pay attention and value these lessons. In order to successfully complete this journey of learning, I have to be a good student of life in our society and the world.

I am talking to so many different people: those who have been in a similar situation and arrived here (United States of America) just like me. I want to let them know that they are not alone. In addition, I want to let others know the similarity of human beings and how many people, like me, have had to endure trials in their life, and they had to work hard to achieve their goal/s or lead a sustainable life for themselves and their families. They must value the enduring journey people like me have had to undertake. I know for sure, to get to where I am today, I had to work twice as hard as many others who have been here before and were born and raised in this country. This memoir is not a history or an opinion. This is my real-life story, which I had to go through day by day. It is the life of a maverick boy who decided to take a totally different route from the rest of his family. Whether it is good or bad, I have been revealing most of my secrets and many different life experiences that I have never spoken about. In some cases, I have been hesitant due to other people's life in order to avoid negative effects or adverse effects on them or their life. Now I hope you will enjoy this real-life story. Thank you, and God bless.

Chapter 1

Innocent Childhood Dream

Birth

I remember when my son, Ari, was born. It was a Saturday night. We were at a wedding party of one of our Kurdish community members (Alan Barzanji was getting married to a Syrian Arab girl). Just after midnight, suddenly, my wife (Aveen) turned to me and gasped, "I am in pain." Right away, I jumped in our car and sped my wife to a nearby hospital. Once there, we were admitted into a secure, clean area surrounded by nurses and doctors. They helped us settle into a nice room with clean beds and crisp white sheets. Soon thereafter, Aveen's whole family showed up and stayed with her from the beginning of the day until we left the hospital. There was good food and plenty of medicine. We were warm and secure. My son was born without incident and was well attended to by doctors and nurses. He was cleaned, bathed, clothed, and returned to us all trussed up in his own bed. I held my newborn American son and thought of his future here. My thoughts soon strayed to my home country, and I thought of my own birth and how different it must have been. It also made me think about birthdays in general and how strange it was for me to consider celebrating my own. When I first came to America, I had to get a check cashed at the bank. When I showed my ID, the clerk smiled and exclaimed, "Happy birthday!" I must have looked like a fool as I just stared at her. She looked down at my ID and asked,

"It is your birthday, right? July first?" I caught on and said, "Oh yes, thank you." It said "July 1" on my ID, but I had never celebrated or even considered my birthday before. I am even pretty sure that it is not even my actual birthday.

The birth of a child was a wonderful occasion for our small Kurdish village of Peerdawood (Peer-da'owd). My own mother had twelve children, and they were all born in our small two-room mud hut. In our culture, when a woman is going to have a baby, friends from the village, her female relatives who live nearby, and her daughters would all pitch in to help. In my case, that would have included my aunt who lived in a one-room hut on our fenced-in property and my older sister from the neighboring village, who was from my father's deceased previous wife. My aunt who lived next door (my father's brother's) and then women of the village who had experience also helped. There were usually several midwives in any village who gave their time as "kher," meaning they volunteered for charity as an act for Allah. Men were never around during childbirth. In fact, most men were out working in the fields and may not have even known their wives were in labor. Small children and the boys were sent out to play, as happened to me many times as my mother gave birth to six more children after me.

When the child was born, they would tightly swaddle it (often so tight it would flatten their skulls). The women and men of the village would gather and celebrate the birth of the child. They would bring food and blankets and such and care for the mother and child for a couple of days. Then life would return to normal. Nobody ever went to the hospital just to have a baby. Since we didn't go to the hospital or fill out paperwork and because very few people could read or write, almost no one kept records of actual birth dates. It was common that many parents weren't even sure what year a child was born, let alone what the actual day was. When I was very young, it was no problem as nobody cared about birthdays, but as I got older, it became increasingly important to have an official date of birth. The first time I really needed it was when I was old enough to attend school.

First Day of School

I remember the first day of school for my son, Ari. My wife and I were so excited. We spent a lot of money to get him ready for the first day: buying clothes, a new schoolbag, new shoes, etc. We were so worried about him. He had never been away from us his whole life. We were a little overprotective of our son since we both were new to this country, so for the whole first day of kindergarten, my wife stayed with him at school to ensure he would be okay. We were so nervous about Ari's first day of school. We made sure he had everything. For weeks after his first day, we would arrive early at the school, often waiting in the car for over an hour because we got there so early, just to make sure Ari didn't miss us when he got out. Our whole extended family here was excited and nervous at the same time about Ari going to school. It was amazing to see how many people in Ari's life cared about his first day of school and how many people were excited to see Ari carrying his schoolbag and facing the new world by himself (well, almost by himself).

When I started school at about age six in Kurdistan, my parents also were engaged in getting me ready, though it was much different for a child in Peerdawood, Kurdistan, in Iraq. There were many preparations to get ready for school. But the process was not nearly as complicated due to the simplicity of our livelihood in the village. We simply didn't have the opportunity to worry about all the things that we worry about in America.

One thing my parents did have to worry about was my official government registration. This created a small issue for Kurdish children who needed to attend school. The Iraqi government wanted to account for all its citizens (especially the males) and wanted records kept on them. So before we could register for school, we needed to have documentation that I was actually a citizen of Iraq. My father had to go into the town of Qushtapa nearby and request my official forms. When they asked for my birth date, he did what almost every mother and father from our region did. He made it up. From his memory, it seemed that I was born in the summer, so he said my birthday was July 1. If he had thought it had been in the winter,

3

I probably would have the birthday of January 1. This was no big deal to me since nobody ever celebrated that day, but if we had celebrated birthdays, there would have been huge birthday celebrations for January 1 and July 1 in our village and throughout Kurdistan.

The morning of my first day of school was finally here, and I could barely contain my excitement. My older sister Gulizar had made a special breakfast for me. She was excited for me to go to school because she knew how much it meant to me. At that time, it was popular and appropriate, culturally, for boys to go to school. At the same time, many girls from the village were in school as well. Nevertheless, it was not required for all of them to attend, and with all the work of housekeeping and my mother having so many small children, my sister decided to stay home and help. My older brother Bakir had also dropped out of school to work in our fields, but my next older brother, Burhan, loved school and stayed. I had the books the school got from the government and had tied them securely with an old belt to keep them together and safe. Then my mother called me over to get clean.

Oh! Such a ritual. Our town was basically dirt. We lived in mud-brick houses, like the ones my older brothers were employed to make. The floors were packed dirt, the yards were packed dirt, the streets were dirt, and the playing fields were grass and dirt. When it rained, our world turned to mud, and when it was dry, dust was everywhere. In a small village where no one had gas lines, electricity, or even running water, it was only natural for a small boy like me to have a nice coating of dirt over my entire body. Bathing was not a daily ritual for anyone in the village. For the most part, it was a weekly task because of the work required to get me passably clean. I was usually happy that we owned our own well to get water because it meant we didn't have to walk to the village center to draw water from the main well, but on bath day, I cursed this convenience because it meant that my mother could use all the water she needed, and for the first day of school, it was not just a cursory cleaning either.

She needed a lot of water! She walked me over to the outside corner of our home where there was at least a little privacy, and then my mother went to it with a will. She took the hard block of soap over to the barrel of near-boiling water. The soap (Sabuni Raqi) smelled so awful—I hated it with all my heart. It looked like it smelled too. It was a sickly yellowish green that looked more like poop from a sick dog than something you should clean with. Unfortunately, it was the cheapest product, and so for us, it was the only type of soap available.

Anxiously, I watched the steam coming off the wash barrel moments before being plunged into it. I felt like I was one of our chickens being boiled alive. She then scrubbed and scraped the layers of dirt from my small frame. The pad she used was made of extremely rough sheep hair. It felt more like a paddle made of little needles puncturing my body. Now I knew what it was like for our birds to be boiled and plucked. My skin was red and stinging, but even my tears would not deter my mother from her focus. Every particle of dirt and grime was peeled off, and from the way I felt, the first few layers of skin came with them. She then combed my hair from a tangled bird's nest into something resembling neatness. Still tingling from my sheering, I dressed gingerly in the same clothing I always wore, but it had also been freshly cleaned. I picked up my new school books; they seemed so heavy. Then I stood for inspection to make sure I was good enough for school.

My mother beamed with pride, and my brothers all said I looked great. My father even smiled at me and told me I would be a great scholar. Guilizar waved to me at the front door while I walked across our yard to the gate entrance to the wall that surrounded our property. I turned around one more time before walking through, but they had already closed the door. What a day this would be!

As I opened the door leading into our village street, rough hands nearly knocked me back in. I heard shouting, and angry soldiers stormed into the yard, practically kicking me out of the way. I scrambled in the dirt on my hands and feet to escape their stomping boots. Our dog, which guarded our property, started up a fierce tirade of barking; and his bared teeth and fangs snapped at the approaching men. One of them pointed his rifle at our dog and shouted something in a weird language to our house. My father came rushing out with a look of fear on his face. He saw me lying in the dirt and the soldier aiming at our dog. He shouted quickly to quiet it, and then the soldiers continued to shout crudely at my father in their strange tongue. He answered them in a hesitant, almost pleading, voice I had never heard from my father before. He was always so sure and powerful. His voice was strong and commanding, and everyone in the village listened to him and respected his advice. Now these rude soldiers were treating him like a peasant with so much disrespect it made me sick, but instead of showing the strong, steady hand I had always seen in him, he cowered before them and just took their verbal abuse.

The soldiers shoved past my father and through my family members who were peering through the doorway, brashly storming into our home. Then they began to search our house. I was not sure what they were looking for or why they were there! Even though it was such a small house, they were very disrespectful. I was so surprised by how they treated our bedding and what little furniture we had. I expected my mother and father would be very upset. If I had ever done anything like that, I would not have been able to sit down for a week. However, both of them just stood there and watched our home be turned inside out. In a little while, after a very violent and thorough search of every single corner of our house (they even looked on the ceiling and floor, possibly to look for guns or contraband material), the soldiers left our house. I was shaking and felt both scared and violated. I had been pushed rudely by men and left unprotected. My father had been yelled at and shamed, my beloved home had been ransacked, and my strong father and stern mother stared silently and could do nothing. I felt bare and empty. The excitement of my first day of school was forgotten, and we all huddled for comfort and protection in our home. After a little while, we got up and started to clean and reorganize our property inside and out.

Suddenly, we heard a series of gunshots behind our house. We all started screaming because it felt so close. We ran back inside, and my mother pulled us to the corner of the room. She felt we would be safe that way. After that, more gunshots and the booming got louder and louder. My father was in the other room, watching our gate through a very small window. I was sitting behind him; it made me feel safer. My father had the Qur'an on his lap. He felt the Qur'an would protect him and his family from the soldiers coming into our house to take him. He believed the Qur'an would make him invisible. My father was praying the whole time. Behind my father, I was watching our gate along with him. We saw two or three soldiers trying to open our gate, and then they started talking and gesturing to each other. They were hesitant to come in, and a second later, they left without coming in.

Soon after, we could hear them yelling at my father's brother, Omer, who lived next door. From the thuds and screams, it sounded like they were hitting him. My father whispered nervously, "They took Omer!" The gunshots, shouting, and ransacking continued from that morning to sunset through our whole village; and for some time after that, the Iraqi military and tanks surrounded the whole village. The brutal beatings left marks on our village that stayed like scars for years. They even left marks on my uncle, who never fully recovered from the interrogation they put him through, and he carried his scarred deformities, both physical and psychological, for the rest of his life.

In my small six-year-old mind, this event completely upended the innocent illusions I had about my family, my community, and my future. I had always taken my safety and security for granted. My father was strong. My brothers were strong, and our family had prestige and honor in our village. I had never considered that I might be in danger from outside influences. Now my sense of security was shattered and not just for my own safety but for my family, my village, and my people. I was born a Kurd and only knew the beauty and traditions associated with it. Now being a Kurd and living in our own land was not as simple as I had assumed. The world outside our village was so suddenly thrust on me that I felt a whirlwind in my mind and heart. The soldiers who were so foreign to me had now made me feel like a foreigner in my own country, in my own village, and even in my own home. They had shown that they were the true masters of our property, and we could do nothing to protest their intrusion into our lives. I was suddenly an outcast and a minority. These soldiers, with their strange clothing and harsh language, were so different; but now I was the one who was different. Our family, all my friends, my teachers, my cousins, our leaders—all of us—were different ones. Just because we were born Kurdish, our government hated us. It even seemed that they wanted to kill us, and we had no freedom whatsoever due to our ethnic identity. The systematic oppression and discrimination that had always existed as an undercurrent in our daily lives that I had never really noticed before was now stark and bleak, as though I might never have freedom again. Now as I moved through my home and village, my eyes started to open, and I started to see the evidence.

The mind of a child seemed to bend and mold around the events of life, like the ground that surrounded our village. There were rocks and rivers, debris, and old machinery that would simply be covered up over time, and soon it was forgotten and remained only as a hill on the landscape. This event, which seemed to form such a poignant mark in my life, was so quickly covered in the mundane day-to-day rituals of life that I cannot even recall if school was canceled that day and, if so, for how long. I just remember that I was soon attending school and learning. For the adults in the village, the event was simply another reminder that they were lesser citizens and to keep their heads down. For us boys, however, it became a legend.

The full truth of what occurred was never revealed or discussed in company. It was only in hushed voices behind closed doors that we would hear about what occurred.

I had always known I was Kurdish, but it had always seemed more like being part of a family. That was just like my last name. Now I started to learn about my heritage. The Kurds, my people, have been fighting for many years for their ancestral homeland, though they have never completely governed it themselves independently in recent history. The men who fight are volunteers from Kurdish villages, cities, and towns. From our village, they were members of the Kurdistan Democratic Party, one of the factions of Kurdish politics. I didn't understand it back then, but it sounded very impressive to my small ears. Most of these men were only boys who had reached an age where they could fight and were determined to free their people. Because we have no government, we never referred to these volunteers as soldiers. That would denote authority and autonomy—two ideals that have been denied to us for millennia. Instead, we call them Peshmerga, which means those "willing to die" in Kurdish.

That day that had started out so promising to me and was shattered in gunfire and violence was because two brothers from our village, who were Peshmerga, were secretly visiting their family. The old men of the village argued about whether the Iraqi military intelligence had information about them or if it was just a random search, and they happened to be there during their routine search for suspicious activities. However, the minute the Iraqi military started searching, the brothers knew they did not have a chance to live; even if they surrendered to the Iraqi military, they would be executed. They decided to fight until they died. As it turned out, only one of the brothers fought until he was martyred. The other still managed to escape unharmed.

Throughout the day, the first boy, Omer, fought and killed more than five soldiers. Finally, he was surrounded, and the Iraqi military killed him. The story everyone told in the village for years was that Omer, the first Peshmerga who fought the Iraqi military, was chased while still fighting for his life. (I used to love recounting his bravery and the cowardice of our enemies that they couldn't stand against one Kurdish boy.) He slipped into a small room, and the military didn't want to lose any more men going in there. The Iraqi military knew where he was in the house, so they brought a tank around to bomb his position. The house was blown apart, but he was still on his feet fighting! (You can imagine how this story would stir the hearts of the young oppressed Kurdish boys in our village.) In the final stage of his fighting, he was shot from behind by the cowards, and so he was killed.

Killing him was not enough for the military, though. Afterward, they dragged his body behind a military truck all the way to the city of Erbil to scare Kurds and make sure to send a message to Kurdish youths, "This is what we are capable of as an Iraqi military!" As for Omer's brother, he was able to hide in some haystacks, and the Iraqi military never found him. He survived, unlike his brother.

From the beginning of that day of fighting, the Iraqi military started taking all males, detained them randomly, and investigated where the Peshmerga were. Despite no one knowing about them, they started violently hurting innocent people and tortured many, including my uncle. My uncle was tortured and dragged with his face on the ground. He was tortured for hours despite any evidence of wrongdoing. When they let him go, you could not recognize him. Blood was smeared all over his face from the cuts and beating. The abuse left scars on his face that were visible until he died. In fact, my uncle never fully recovered physically or mentally throughout his life as a result of this Iraqi military action. He was innocent and, in his whole life, had never hurt anyone or tried to do anything unlawful. Nevertheless, he and many others like him became victims of this outrageous atrocity.

This was one of the crucial points in my life. I had seen first-hand the brutality, oppression, cruelty, and total disregard that the government had for me, my family, my relatives, my village, and my people. This event forever seared in my mind an apprehension for the government but also a defiance of what they were trying to do to our people. Instead of putting fear into my heart by their brutality and murder, it inspired me and many other boys. We saw the two boys as heroes. They had stood up to a mighty, hateful force. One had survived, and the other was a martyr. He was a true Peshmerga for giving up his life for our people. This event affected me tremendously as a young boy and later on, as a youth, made me write poetry for Omer because he had earned so much respect from the bottom of my heart.

I guess it's not so strange then that I carefully watched my son walk to school and was there to pick him up well before it was time. I know people in this country take security and safety for granted, but where I came from, things were different. Those basic human rights you expect to be sacred to you every day simply ceased to exist in our world. Our property, our words, and even our bodies were not guaranteed to us. Safety and security were dreams that only existed in fantasy. Above all, the dignity of human beings was being daily overrun and crushed by the government. So today, though I know we are safe and live in a land where all the citizens have rights to property and safety, old wounds still flare up now and then, and it's difficult to forget them.

My Elementary School

Despite the terrible events that engulfed our village on the day I was to start school, I eventually did get to go to school. Once the confusion died down and our lives returned somewhat to normal, I started my education. Though there were many atrocities by the regime, there were some positive things that the government did for us. The government built our school in the village. It was made of stones and cement (one of the only structures, besides the mosque, with an actual floor and not just dirt). The school had six classrooms and one room which all the teachers and principal shared. The classroom was furnished with wooden chairs and tables. We had a blackboard in the front of each room and a small stove, which was used during the winter to keep students warm. It ran on the kerosene-type fuel we all used. Classes were located all on one side of the building, like a hallway. Each room was facing the other.

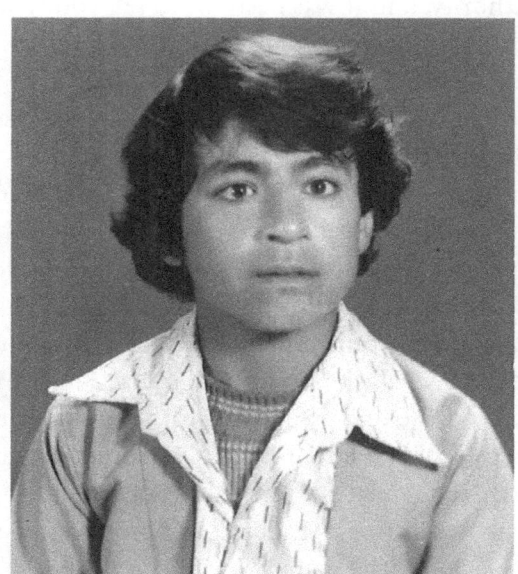

Dr. Bewar Kamal—young age

11

Our school system was designed similarly to a military camp system. At specific times, we were expected to be in our seats, at full attention, waiting for the teacher to begin. When we were dismissed, we were expected to quickly exit the room. I enjoyed learning, but one thing I did not miss was the way our teachers treated us. Just like in a military camp, the teachers were usually very strict and often very cruel. Many of our teachers saw no reason to remain composed about their job and kids. There were some good teachers in the lot; however, the vast majority of them treated us very harshly. We were often insulted, mocked, hit, and sometimes even beaten by a teacher for minor infractions of the rules or common mistakes in our learning. If you did a calculation wrong, you were publicly shamed by the teacher for not studying hard enough. I can remember countless times when I was cuffed or smacked for simple mistakes or talking to friends. It was just the system of the time, and we could expect no help from our parents. In that time period, a child could be beaten by those in authority, and it was best not to tell your parents you got in trouble as it could mean a second beating at home.

I remember one time during recess, when I was playing with my friends in the classroom and running over the desks. I was having so much fun that I missed that recess was over. I was facing my friends and jumping, making faces with them, when suddenly they became very quiet. I did not realize Mamosta Nuri, our teacher, had just walked into the classroom. Still standing on the desk, I turned around and saw him coming toward me with his stick in his hand. Usually, I would take my punishment without a fuss, but between the fire in his devilish eyes and my knowledge that I had really crossed a line this time, I did the only thing that came to my mind. I ran. He started chasing me over and around the desks, swiping at me when he got close. He struck me several times, seeming to find the parts of my small body that would sting the most, the bony places, such as knees, elbows, and back. This scenario continued to play out for several minutes before he had had enough. He stopped and called for attention. I meekly halted, and he stood panting in irate frustration. My knees trembled, and I wondered if I would be allowed to say goodbye to my mother and father before I was executed. He commanded me to approach him and display both my hands opened, palms up. He took his striking rod and then commenced hitting my bare skin. He struck each hand five times, and they stung like fire. Through clenched teeth, he breathed, "Do not ever run over the desks again." After that incident, I never misbehaved again, at least not when he could catch me doing it. I know for sure, though, as a young student, I was one of the hell of terror. Few of the other teachers could control me. But I am still not sure I deserved such a harsh punishment, nor do I believe that it served to make me a better student.

My Cool Bicycle

Recently, I was able to buy a Tesla. My son loves it and fully expects to get one when he is older. In the meantime, I have bought him bikes, scooters, rollerblades, really anything that he sees that he might want to ride around on I can get for him. His mother and I, to some extent, get him anything he desires. We do not want him to take his lifestyle for granted. We want him to appreciate his many blessings, so sometimes when he asks for something, we say no. The guilt of saying no to Ari, however, makes my wife and me feel so depressed. We remember the poverty of our childhoods and not having anything. Now that we can afford it, we want to give him everything, but as they say, this is "tough love." Yeah, we are not so good at this. However, despite all that, I think back to my childhood and struggle just to get a bike.

Though my father was a respected and prominent man in our village of Peedawood, we were still poor compared to the rest of the country, though we had enough food and we all had clothing. We had no idea all the things we simply did not have. There was no electricity until many years later, so no TVs, radios, or video games. No sports equipment, board games, new shoes, comic books. Our land was fertile, but the government suppression of the Kurdish people meant that we could never achieve prominence. When I was young, we didn't even have indoor plumbing. No gas or running water, no paved roads. Most villagers had to draw water from the main well in the center of town. We might listen to the radio at the cantina near the main highway for entertainment, but that was all. Some people owned cars and trucks (my brother Mohammed even owned a Land Rover, but that's another story). For the most part, people walked or rode donkeys and mules to get around. We had an old mule that we rode around as well. It taught me more cuss words than I probably should have known as a child; he was so stubborn that even a strong stick would not get that beast to move when he didn't want to. My older brothers owned a motorbike that they used to get to work and school, but I could never use it. I was really left to simply walk places if I wanted to get there.

As a child, I dreamed about having my own bicycle. I remember how I bothered my father every single day to buy me one. I knew my father always paid extra attention to me because of our bond. I knew he loved me very much, so he would never say no. However, he had no money either, so to postpone my request, he said that I should "First, try to learn how to ride the 'bike.' Then we will talk about it."

We had an old "bike" at our house, but it was not operational. The chain was old, rusty, and bent in so many places it looked like an old, knotted red rope. The tires were also shoddy, and the seat was only a seat in name and probably would have given me tetanus if I had tried to sit on it. Fortunately, it was so high up that I couldn't have sat on it, even if it was a nice seat. I was determined, though, to show my father I was serious. I have always had a strong, persistent will (some would call it stubbornness, and my mom would probably say "stupid obstinance"). I was a lot like our donkey in that way. I simply saw this as the next step to getting what I wanted. I started by trying to fix the bike up to be operational. I started with the chain, but when I put it on the chain cog, the chain actually just broke apart. The wheels were another issue. They were both flat, and I didn't have a pump. Fortunately, I really didn't even realize that the tires needed air. There was obviously nothing to be done about the height. To some, this may have been as far as they got, and I'm sure my father hoped the same, but in my mind, I could overcome it all.

First, I patched and tied the chain back together with a piece of metal and a tiny rope (I thought I had done brilliantly); triumphantly, I put it loosely around the cog. I gingerly stepped over the middle bar and tried to balance while putting my feet on the pedals. Now that I got a good look at them, I realized they might pose a problem as well. They were old, cracked, and broken; so it was difficult to keep my feet on the paddles. Between balancing, slippery pedals, and a terrible seat (I could not sit on the saddle because there was no way I could reach the pedals if I did), I still could not reach the lowest point of the cycle. I didn't worry about this and assumed I would just use the pedal on the other side. I positioned myself precariously on the bar, shoved off, and started to try to pedal. However, I found that method would not work very well. Every time I started pedaling, the chain simply fell apart (so much for my ingenuity). Obviously, I did not have the professional skill of repairing bike chains. This, however, was simply another obstacle that I would have to get around before I showed my father that I could learn to ride a bike.

There was a little hill outside of the south gate of our yard that dipped down into a gully for a small stream to run around the back of our village. When I reflect on it, the downhill stretch seemed so big that it felt like a huge mountain and the river running through a deep gorge. In reality, it was only a small hill. Nevertheless, I figured I could use the descent from the hill to teach myself biking without bothering to pedal.

At the top of the hill, I looked back to see my house. I could see the edge of our property and the top of our mosque. I just imagined myself riding my brand-new bike through the village and how my friends would all point and the elders would congratulate me. I couldn't wait to get started.

The little hill behind our house fell into a ditch on the far side. Some children are born with a sense of caution. They avoid the dark and don't get too close to the edges. I never had that. From a young age, I was fearless. It must have had something to do with my stubborn determination; pain was just something that wouldn't get in the way of my ultimate goals. This would serve me well later when I was hot, dehydrated, and starving during a long battle or freezing and sick in a refugee camp. Now it just meant a lot of pain.

The hill looked so steep to me, which only proved in my mind that it would work. I knew I would be able to get up some good speed. Well, the bike went down the hill just fine, but the problem was me getting down the hill at the same time as the bike. It always seemed that I would start out on top of the bike, but at some moment in the descent, the bike would be on top of me, and then it would leave me there all bruised and dusty halfway up the hill and go careening down the rest of the way by itself into the dry riverbed. No matter how many times I found myself under the cycle, however, I still jumped back up and pushed it back to the top to ride back down. I am not sure which was the worst part: falling off into the dirt and rocks or retrieving the bike and pushing it slowly up the hill on its flat tires.

I repeated this process over and over for hours whenever I had free time. This went on for days and weeks, but I was determined to ride that bike even if it killed me. Which it almost did. One day, I was going downhill, and the wind was whipping my hair and clothes. I still could not reach the pedals to control my feet. There were no real brakes (I didn't know that bikes had such safety features), but I figured I was used to falling, so it didn't matter that I was going so fast. Suddenly, I hit a rock, and the bike flipped over on top of me. I remember being under the bike and knowing that I had hurt my neck very badly. I still got up and tried to act like it was no big deal. It was pretty bad the first day, but I figured it would be all right in the morning. Instead, it steadily got worse. For days, I was not able to move my neck very well. After a few days, when my mother or brother called me, I had to turn my whole little body to talk to them. Of course, there was no doctor to go to or hospital to check me out and see what was going on with me or where I had been hurt. We simply hoped that it would eventually go away like everything else always did. This didn't, however. The suffering and pain in my neck continued for weeks and even worsened.

Finally, my mother was tired of seeing me suffer and complain, so she decided to do something about it. She told me she was going to take me to get it fixed. All that night, I thought I would go to the city, and maybe if I were lucky, I would get some kebab for lunch. Well, I thought wrong. Instead of walking to the highway to flag down a car or taxi, we started walking in the other direction. My mother walked me to the outskirts of our village—out past my school to a lady named Khyree. Since they lived on the other side of the village, they were far from our home, so we did not have that close of a relationship. I knew her children from school, and sometimes, they came when we played soccer, but I didn't really know anything about her "doctor" skills. My mother told me that Khyree knew how to fix my neck. Who knows how she obtained that skill, but my mother trusted her enough to hand me over to Khyree to fix my neck. Since I trusted my mother, I went along. I really had no choice. By this time, I was moving like a stiff robot.

The pain was so bad; it was hard to move straight. My mother, holding my hand, walked me into their gate. Khyree was a good-looking lady in her black dress. She had a cigarette between her fingers and asked my mother what was wrong with little Kamal. Well, my mother started in and told her the whole story. Khyree went back to her home, sat on her Kurdish rug, and invited my mother and me to come in and have a seat. We sat down, I was next to my mother, and she said, "Come over, son. Let me see what is going on with you." I could not even look at her straight. She motioned for me to sit right in front of her. I eased myself down across from her, but I was not able to look straight at her anymore because of the crick in my neck. It felt like my neck had turned ninety degrees to the other side of my body, and it simply couldn't look straight forward anymore. She became more stern and almost demanding, asking me over and over again to look straight at her; but try as I might, I could not! I finally forced all my will and tried my hardest to move just my neck. As soon as I did this to try to look at her, I saw her big right hand streaking toward my face. She slapped me across my face as hard as she could! I was so scared I jerked my head back really quickly and felt something pop. Suddenly, I could move my head! I started twisting it this way and that. It felt so wonderful! After a minute or so of me moving around, she asked me how I felt. At first, I felt sore and in a little pain, but it was such a relief to move it again. We worked at it for a while, and by the time I left, I was moving straight. My neck got much better after that without ever seeing a real doctor.

I think about how today when I hurt my neck or back, I am able to visit a licensed chiropractor or massage therapist. They have nice offices, professional beds, and sterilized tools in air conditioning. Their licenses are framed on the wall, and I did not have to get slapped to get better. For some reason as well, it takes a lot longer to get through the healing process and costs a lot more. I am not sure, though, that they are any more qualified than my neighbor Khyree.

You would think this would be a learning experience for me and that I would give up trying to ride a bike. No way! That was my dream—to learn how to bike, and I would not give up. Besides, I knew that I could just get help if I hurt myself again. That bicycle had become a symbol for me. It was more than just a toy that I could ride around on. I had worked too hard for it. It was a symbol of freedom, prosperity, and determination. I could not give up now that I had come so far. I would have that bike.

I continued my solitary effort with the broken bike. Soon thereafter, Aziz, my neighbor who was the same age, decided to join me when he saw that I was not giving up. We soon were both riding and crashing down our hill, but this time, we had each other to critique and give advice. Slowly, it got easier to ride the bike. But still, I was only using the hill to give me momentum. The pedals were basically only used for show. I pedaled, of course. But without a chain, it really did absolutely nothing for me, and I couldn't even get my short legs through the whole pedal cycle.

As my balance improved, I knew I was getting better at riding a bike. Each night, I would give my family updates on my improvements. I reminded my father often of his promise and pestered him to know when he would buy me a bike.

Every time my father went to the city, I would ask him if he would be bringing me my bicycle this time. As was his custom, he would never say no; he did not want to hurt my feelings. Being the child I was, I did not even consider the impact such a gift might have on a family our size. Our family was very big, and we had very little money. If he bought me a bike, what would all my brothers think! Could he even have offered it to me or them? These are the questions that I did not ask. I was so self-centered and focused that I did not even consider those thoughts. So every time he came back from the city, I would run up to him and ask about my bike. He would smile and say, "It is still in the process to put your bike together, son." He would get creative about how long it took to add handlebars or get the balance right or hook up the chain or pump the tires. "Do not worry. I will get it for you."

I am not sure how he did it, but he must have been saving and looking for a long time. It took my father more than a year, but he was true to his word. One day when he came home, he had a bright shiny bicycle with him. The joy of my voice must have echoed through the whole village when I saw my father with my bike. The joy of finally getting that bike was one of the happiest memories of my life. I have never been so excited about getting anything in my whole life. The bike itself was nothing fancy. It was most likely refurbished, and there were no special gears or anything, but it was mine, and I had worked and suffered so much to get it. It was a lesson I learned well, that if you work and suffer and never give up, you can have whatever you desire. Years later, after living in the United States, I bought a brand-new Tesla; but even such a beautiful new powerful car did not give me as much joy as seeing my father holding my first bicycle.

I have many great memories of that bicycle. I still had to learn how to ride it. I wasted no time jumping on to figure it out. I rode it day and night, and as it was a poor village, most of the other kids didn't have bikes, so I would let my friends try riding it as well. I believe riding a bike is hard for those who do not know how to ride it and don't have anyone to explain the mechanics to them. Here in America, it seems that every child has a bike, and every adult knows how to ride, so there is always someone to guide, but without a teacher, it took me quite some time to master it. I will never forget an incident a few days after I got my bike. I was just riding around the mosque, and it was afternoon. I was just figuring out how to really get the pedals going to build up speed, yet I had not really ever learned to turn. On the hill, we always just went straight down. Moving the handlebars had always resulted in painful accidents, so I had only ever just held the front wheel steady. As I was enjoying my new bike, one of the elders of the community, his name was Mam Shera, was coming out from the mosque after praying. As he exited the gate from the mosque, I was on a straight line directly toward him. I didn't know how to turn or how to break. I only knew how to crash. I could not stop or turn the bike another way. I landed directly between his legs. He started cursing and yelling at me, "Are you blind, child?" He screamed, "Cannot you see me?" I just sat there in fearful shock as the full force of his curses pounded down on me. I could not say anything as I slowly extricated myself from his legs and pants and the various parts of my bike. I mumbled a hasty apology and quickly left with him, still swearing about kids in general and sending curses toward me, "I hope you will be blinded!"

I eventually got the hang of turning and breaking and spent many years biking around our small village, sharing my bike with all my friends and maybe even sometimes with my brothers. At such an early age, learning how to ride a bike was helpful and served me well because, years later, my father registered and ordered a new motorcycle from the government for our family. I then got the chance to drive a motorbike, and learning how to drive was much easier (and safer) than learning to cycle. Luckily, I did not break any of my bones, and I did not hurt myself in the process. One funny thing I never forget about the process is that I was so young and short when I started learning to ride the motorcycle; I could not balance the bike when I came to a full stop. As a result, I had to jump off and out while the motorcycle was still moving and still hold on to it, so it wouldn't fall over and crash. Often, I would get dragged or crushed by the motorcycle that kept going or fell over on me.

As for buying stuff for my son, I did learn a lot from working hard to earn my bike, but now I am able to give my son both the time and materials so we can spend time enjoying the blessings of my work. Maybe the system is not perfect, but I am so thankful for how it turned out.

Childhood in a Village

My home

Ari grew up in the suburbs. We live in a cul-de-sac connected to a main road run by fast food, department stores, grocery stores, and businesses. He takes the bus to school and bikes to the parks to play ball. We recognize our neighbors for the most part and wave at them when we pass them on occasion. We live so close together, though, but I still feel like I am a stranger in a crowd. I don't really know anyone who passes on the roads, and I have to travel miles to get to somebody that I really know. We may have all the modern conveniences of technology and commercialism, but sometimes, I feel like everyone I meet is all alone in an overcrowded urban city.

It was such a small village that I was born into. I can remember standing on the roof of our one-floor home and being able to see my whole village. Each of the families owned a small plot of land, about an acre for their home. Each plot of land had a wall about a meter and a half high (five to six feet) that went around their property. This was to provide a little privacy and to keep the animals secure. The land we lived on had two gates, one from the north, which led into the center of the village, and the other one from the south of our house, which was more connected to the outside of the village toward our farmland. My father had built an awning at the entrance that was shaded and nice to stand under to wait when others came to visit before they came onto our property. (That was where I had been when the soldiers had shoved me back into our property on my first day of school.) Our poultry coop was next to the gate on the wall, and our outhouse stood next to the coop; we didn't get plumbing until years later when we moved into the city.

Our house was on the far wall near the south entrance. It was a very simple dwelling made with mud bricks and a wooden roof. The back wall was actually the back wall of our property. The south entrance had a large opening for carts and later for my brother Mohammed's SUV so he could keep it secure. On our property, we had also built an additional one-room home for my aunt. Her husband had died, and without a husband, she and her daughter would have been destitute if my father had not welcomed her to our plot.

Just behind the homes, most villagers kept their animals. We did as well. We had sheep and goats, a dog, chickens, turkeys, ducks, and geese, along with various other pets. My older brother Bakir owned some domesticated doves. They were beautiful, and I remember how hard he guarded those doves against stray cats to keep them from being eaten. I remember one time he became so mad because he kept losing doves. You could see the evidence of the crime by scattered feathers everywhere from the feral cats enjoying their prey. My brother could get really angry when he was cheated, and he felt cheated right then. He decided that he was going to get even with those cats for killing his pets. He was very young, not even a teenager, but he got my father's old shotgun out and decided he was going to ambush those cats. He had blood in his eyes as he waited hours and hours to blast the criminal felines. Every time they showed their guilty faces, he fired at the wall around our home. They were good strong mud bricks, and the pellets did little more than pepper the outside. He never successfully killed any cats, but at least for a little while, cats were too scared to come near his doves. Eventually, he tired of taking care of the birds. Like most boys, he got interested in other things. He sold some of them, and others he freed to fly wherever they wanted, and they left forever.

My eldest brother was already married and owned a home next to our property. In fact, we shared the same back entrance where he could park. He had a real Land Rover. It was his pride and joy as very few people own cars in our small village. It was parked next to our small garden that supplied vegetables for our diet and where we kept our farm cart that was pulled by our old donkey.

Though the house we lived in was simple, it was no different from anyone else in our village: mud-brick house with a wooden roof and dirt floor. In America, when you say "two rooms," people think that it has two bedrooms; and they don't count the kitchen, living room, garage, and bathroom. No, it was very modest and consisted of two rooms which functioned as our dining room, parlor, living room, and bedrooms depending on what we needed. The rooms were not even that big. They were about four meters long and three meters wide (twelve feet by ten feet). All the houses in the village were the same, except many of them had only one room. They were built with bricks made from straw and mud, with common mud used as well for the mortar to enhance its strength and for insulation during hard, cold winters. When I got older, I actually learned to make these bricks myself. Though they kept heat in for the winter, this meant they were too hot in the summertime, so most of the villagers would sleep on the roof. It was cooler to sleep outside since no air-conditioning system existed. I loved lying on my back, watching the stars and listening to the night noises. It was so peaceful; I miss that a lot.

There was no kitchen in our home. In fact, we didn't have running water or electricity at all when I was young. We did our cooking just outside the house. We had a gas stove that ran on fuel that was similar to kerosene. This was our main source of power for cooking, hot water, heat in the winter, and light at night. My mother and sisters did most of the cooking, and usually, we just ate outside. Most often, we had food that we had grown or traded for in the village. We ate a lot of goats and sheep. Also, we had chicken and turkey. We raised all these animals ourselves for our own food. We also ate seasonal vegetables from our garden and small farm plot, as well as bread that my mother made. She made bread every morning. Sometimes, she put fresh homemade cheese inside while it baked and added sesame seeds to the top. Those were the best days!

When you entered the house through the small wooden door, you walked into the front room. In the house, the floor was hardened dirt, but my mother kept it as clean as she could. In the corner, I remember, there was a very simple shelf that was placed in the corner. The shelf held all our bedding for the evening. The shelf was where we stored pillows, blankets, and small mattresses called *doshak* to sit or sleep on. In the winter, my mother also kept *jajim*, a Kurdish handmade blanket made from goat hair (it was very itchy and felt like thorny weeds on your body). It was warm but so uncomfortable that you had to debate what was worse: freezing to death or death by a thousand scratches. My father once bought a bunch more of them that were store-bought from Erbil. Since ours were homemade,

23

I assumed that real store-bought blankets would be much more comfortable. I was sorely disappointed. They were just as itchy and pokey as the homemade ones we already had. Even though we lived on dirt, my mother always tried to keep our bedding as neat and clean as possible, so she used to drape a sheet over the shelf while our bedding was not being used to keep the dirt and dust off it.

I am not sure how old the house was; but our family, my grandfather, had the house built when he was granted land by the government. The land we had in town was big enough for our family. However, our small house did not have enough rooms to fit everyone. My family was big! We were ten siblings (two of my siblings had died when they were only babies) living in this small, simple house. I remember that one of the rooms was designated for my parents, girls, and younger siblings; and the other room was for older male siblings, such as my older brothers and me. My brothers and I slept next to each other on *doshak*, all lined up in the same room when it became too cold to sleep on the roof. As a child, I was filled with a sense of family and closeness, and I enjoyed such an environment while I was growing up. However, as I grew, I started craving a little privacy, and I even secretly dreamed of my own room. For my father, it was an impossible thing to be able to offer each of us a room. We had no money to construct more rooms, so that was all we had, and it was always crowded.

Sometimes, it was even more crowded. Most people only traveled by walking or riding donkeys, so if they came to visit from a different village, they were not able to return home until the next day. In our culture and area, when people came to visit, which seemed to constantly happen, it was always expected that you would invite them into your home and feed them and give them a place to sleep before they would return the next day or after a short, extended stay. So when we hosted visiting family or guests, our crowded two-room home fairly burst, and those were especially the nights when my brothers and I would sleep on the roof. Of course, that would only happen during the summertime or early fall, when it was not cold outside. When I became a teenager, I remember how hard I wished for my own room and my own place. I look at how my own son lives now, and it seems a world apart from what I grew up with.

My community

Besides the land we had in the village, we had some land in the surrounding countryside as well. My father was a farmer and had about twenty-five hectares of land, which was given to his father by the government in 1958 during Abd al-Karim Qasim's regime.

Of course, I did not know this information until I was older when I started to learn about the history of Iraq and Kurdistan. The way that my grandfather acquired the land and what he was able to do with it changed the course of my family's fortune.

My son, Ari, loves to play, especially basketball, and he wants to play all the time. But he is always watched and guarded when he goes out. Because of the busy roads with cars, unknown strangers, and different cultures that surround us, he has never been allowed to just roam free. When he was young, his mother and aunts would take him to the park. I would take him to play basketball. We knew where he was at all times and were very careful about his safety. My childhood was nothing like that at all.

My home village was called Peerdawood (Peer-da'owd). In the early '70s, when I was young, it consisted of only thirty to forty families; many of which were our relatives. The village is located in northern Iraq in the Erbil province on a flat plateau (Erbil is the Iraqi name of the Kurdish city Hawler, the capital city for the Kurdistan Regional Government). The region I grew up in has always been well known throughout history for its arable land and bountiful harvests. Historically, this area was called the cradle of civilization because it lies between the Tigris and Euphrates Rivers. We were much closer to the Tigris, and in fact, one of the larger tributaries called the "Great Zab" or "Upper Zab" flowed right near Erbil, and memories of it played into much of my youth. As such, our land has always been a prosperous farming community.

We lived very close to the major highway that led directly to the capital only ten to twelve kilometers away. Tragically, Peerdawood was razed to the ground in 1988 while I was fighting as a Peshmerga rebel, by Saddam's regime during the Anfal campaign. It was rebuilt in a fashion after 1992 when the first Kurdish Regional Government was established in Kurdistan of Iraq, but it is not the same as the village I grew up in. I remember one time I was visiting my family and went to see the old village where I grew up. To me, the village was not the same at all. Everything was different from my childhood memories. The homes were new construction with electricity and indoor plumbing. People were driving cars, and it just felt busier. I did not recognize the place where I spent most of my childhood.

In our small village, the streets were just packed dirt. The twenty or so properties that made up the community were constructed roughly in a horseshoe shape around the center of town, where the community water well was easy to access for anyone. We didn't have electricity or plumbing in our community until many years later. The well was run by a machine which ran on kerosene-type fuel and supplied many families with water. Fortunately for my family, we owned our own well on our property, so we didn't have to carry it all the way from the center of the village.

There were two small cafés at the entrance of the village right next to the highway (we called them casinos—in Kurdish *chaixana*—or teahouses). The men of the village would gather there to play *dama* (a game similar to checkers) or dominoes and talk about the news of the town and the country. We would go there, too, when we had a little money for candy or soda, but it was rare that we would have extra money. If we went there, it was just to watch the older men of the village play games, talk about problems, or discuss politics.

There was a small dirt field on the outskirts of the village near my home where all the boys nearby would go after school to play soccer. We had cheap plastic balls to play with, but we would still play for hours. Sometimes, groups of boys from neighboring villages would come to play against us because we had an actual state-sponsored school building with a great field to play on. We would also go to the other villages sometimes, but more often than not, they would come to us. Soccer was our life as boys. We would play all day until we could no longer see the ball unless it was a full moon, and then we would still play late into the evening. I don't remember ever having a curfew. I just got home when I got home, and that was life. It was very safe in our village (aside from the Iraqi military, but they rarely came to small villages like they had when I started school). Everyone knew everyone else, and everyone knew everyone else's business as well.

Soccer wasn't just big for the children. Most of the villagers would listen to soccer matches on battery-powered radios, but we never watched them since we had no TVs. It wasn't until years later that television arrived in our village. I remember one of the first houses that got a TV was my friend Tofiq's family. My first glance at a live TV was late after sunset. There was a whole group of boys. We were all outside their gates, drawn by the bright flashing lights from their window. We just stood there staring at the small little screen. It was so small outside their gates, through their window that we could barely make out any characters it showed, but we stood there none-theless, fascinated by what we saw as though it was coming from a much farther distance. Now, in my memory, that small beacon of the future stands in stark contrast to the dirt streets, mud-brick homes, and farm animals scattered throughout the neighborhood. It was a call from another world and a distant future.

That TV, however, didn't come for many years, so we were content to simply listen to the soccer matches on the radio. We all knew about the great soccer players, though, even famous ones from around the world. I grew up idolizing the Brazilian soccer player "Pele," though we pronounced his name wrong; we always said "Bele." We had soccer cards with players' pictures, and sometimes we played with them. Most of these cards we had were the Iraqi national soccer team players, such as Falah Hassan and Adnan Drjal, who were some of the more famous ones.

We preferred to play at the school, as I said, since they had real soccer balls and a better field, but it was usually too far from our house to easily meet there. Our school was new. It was built by the government as part of a community outreach program. We had desks, chalkboards, and an actual cement floor (as I said, most of the buildings and homes, including mine, were just packed dirt and handmade bricks). The school was on the far side of town but still not very far at all because it was such a small village. It was very easy to walk there every day with all the other kids who decided to go to school in the village.

The school was all government funded, so they provided breakfast and lunch. I always looked forward to this because we got fruit and dairy products, which we rarely got at home. In the morning, the farash (the school security guard), whose name was Mam Saeed, which means "Uncle Saeed," with his wife Safya, would boil cow's milk (which was rare in our region) so we could get a cup of warm milk when we got to school. The fruit might even be a banana or an apple! They also provided the school books and materials for our classes, which was nice, but all the material was exactly the same throughout the country for each grade. All the material was approved and published by the Iraqi Ministry of Education, so it was very heavy on teachings of Arabic and Islam and history according to Arabian Iraqi tradition. It was in school that I learned Arabic since everyone in my village spoke Kurdish as a primary language, as they still do today in that region.

In America, I hear about problems in school between students. Bullying is always a hot topic. It was the same in my school. The way I dealt with my bully, though may be different from how I would advise my own son, gives a strong impression of my personal nature. I remember one of the boys who claimed to be my friend Aziz (Aza, as we called him).

He was bigger than many of the other kids in our grade and liked to bully many kids. A couple of times, that bullying included me since I was a small skinny boy. For the breakfasts at school, we used to get a piece of cheese, along with hot milk and fruit. I was not a big fan of the cheese, so sometimes, Aziz would ask me to give him my cheese. It was not a big deal at first, but he kept asking for my cheese, and it soon became a demand. Even though I didn't really like my cheese, I didn't think that he should just automatically assume that I had to give him mine. That scenario was repeated a few times, however, and I got sick of it. One day, as we were eating breakfast outside the school, he came up and demanded my piece of cheese. I looked at him and told him that I wanted my cheese today and that he couldn't have it. Surprised and a little insulted, he insisted that he wanted it so I better give it to him. I was scared and knew that he bullied other children for things he wanted, so I gave it to him, not wanting to start anything. It happened again the next day, and I meekly handed over my cheese. Inside, however, I had a terrible sick feeling. I wondered if I was a coward. I wondered why someone could be so cruel that they would want to push other people around. I had difficulty eating my other food I felt so sick. Finally, I decided I would not give him my cheese again. The next day, during the lunch hour, Aziz asked for the cheese again. I steadied my nerves, knowing that I had to tell him no. This time, I aggressively stood up in front of him. He was still taller, but I stretched myself and firmly said no in a slightly louder voice than I had planned. He must have seen this as a challenge to his authority, so he looked at my small frame and shoved me, trying to push me back down. "Yes, you will give me that cheese," he sneered. I stubbornly held my ground, and I pushed him back and said no again. Then something inside me snapped. I knew I was smaller and couldn't win a fight with him. My teachers did not care about us as children, and if we went for help, we would either be mocked or beaten. I only had myself. My eyes were burning, and my heart was beating as though I had just finished a soccer match. I was so furious that he would continue to bully me. I looked around the empty lot and saw a fair-sized rock. I quickly picked it up and swung my fist with the stone. It hit him right on the head. He fell down and started crying and swearing at me. I was still full of rage, and seeing him on the ground now made me want to pummel him after he had fallen. I started to run toward him because I wanted to kick him so badly. Fortunately for both him and me, some of my fellow class-mates came between us and stopped me. My blood pressure eased, and my mind started to relax. I now saw him clearly. He was bleeding on his head from where I had struck him. He started mumbling, this time quietly to himself, surprised and now a little scared of me.

He never bothered me after that incident. In fact, as a result of my defense, Aziz started to be more friendly to me. As we got older, we did become good friends, and he was not so quick to attack kids smaller than him, though he continued to get us in trouble. But that was the school I attended in my childhood.

Finally, as with every town in the Middle East, we had a mosque which stood at the head of the town on the edge of the horseshoe, away from the well. From the top of the mosque would echo the call to which we would wake each morning. Listening to the call to prayer being sung to us five times was simply how the world was. The task of calling to prayer was not the specific job of any one person, and for young boys, it was exciting if they could get the chance to do it.

I remember one time in particular, after electricity had been set up in our village, perhaps when I was about twelve, my friend Aziz and I were both given the chance to sing the call to prayer. We were wrestling over the microphone to see who would finally get the chance. He was still bigger than me, so he finally won out and took the microphone. At the hour, he solemnly held the microphone and, in his young voice, boomed the call to the whole village. I was upset that I had lost and was pouting until a few minutes later when his father and several prominent members of the community showed up at the mosque, looking fairly upset.

We had been so excited about our chance to call that we had misjudged the time by a whole hour. He was scolded and ridiculed terribly for his mistake, but I was just grateful that he had been the one who got the mic while I had escaped embarrassment. This became a famous incident in our village, and my dad said that the elders of the village were complaining about how embarrassing it was that small children were controlling the mosque and calling for prayer; and they specifically changed my friend's name, which was Aziz, to Aza, which was an insulting abbreviation because he had set himself up as an elder in our community and brought shame on them all.

My young days were spent in such frivolities as the time sped in front of me. Weeks seemed like hours, hours seemed minutes, and moments in time seemed to last forever. But that village, and that life I so loved, is now completely lost to the passage of time and the ravages of war.

Brick Making and Kiln

Ari, my son, is an only child. He also has almost no responsibility. Of course, he has to clean his room and help with housework here and there. He has homework to do, but he really has no responsibility. I am so grateful for this fact. He will be able to enjoy his childhood to its fullest. My own childhood ended early, and even when I had lots of freedom to play, I also always had chores to keep our home going.

When I was about ten, Bakir, my older brother who seemed to always be working and planning, had been in some deep conversations with my mother. They must have been about me because they always stopped when I came too close.

"He's too young," I would overhear my mother say.

"He will be perfect, and we need the money, Mom," I would hear him reply.

As it turned out, they were talking about me. Bakir and Burhan, my older brothers, had both been hired by a local brickmaker to work when the rains had stopped and the sun was hot enough. I didn't know that we didn't have enough money. I had everything I wanted, even a bike. We had plenty of food, a strong house, and animals. I didn't realize how hard my father and brothers worked just to provide all this and how tenuous the situation was depending on the growing season and our crops.

To me, a paying job sounded good for other reasons; it would be nice to be able to buy candies and soda at the casino where we went to listen to the news or watch sports. My mother did not have much sway in the family at any rate, and my father could see that Bakir had a good head for economics and usually listened to his son's advice. So I soon found myself being woken up early in the morning, handed a scrap of food, and being crushed between my two older brothers on Bakir's small motorbike.

Bakir, who was about sixteen or seventeen, drove and took the brunt of the cold morning air that froze his cheeks and hands. Burhan, about fourteen or fifteen, sat in the back and held onto my brother in front of me as tightly as possible while freezing his fingers just to protect me from falling off. I could barely breathe and got so stiff from sitting between them for the long ride, but I didn't dare move my head or hands out from between the coats because it seemed like it was the only pocket of warmth left in the world.

My mother, it turned out, was right to be concerned about me. We spent hours stomping barefoot in mud and straw to form the mixture that would be put into the molds. The water was cold on my small bare feet, and the mud was sticky and got very deep. I remember many times that I would get so slogged down that I couldn't extract my small toes from the mud holes, and my brothers would have to come over and rescue me.

Besides the stickiness, the mud was littered with debris such as branches, briers, and old broken glass and metal. It hurt so bad to stomp down onto a sharp thorn, which would usually result in falling into the mud completely. Sometimes, though, if it was very cold, my feet would be numb, and I wouldn't realize the damage I had done to my feet until much later.

After mixing the mud, we then had to haul it over to be formed into bricks. We spent our days stomping, hauling, and molding the bricks into long neat rows. As the weather got hotter and the bricks hardened, it was time to put them in the kiln. The bricks were carefully stacked in the large oven on our employer's land. We would stack and stack and stack them. I could only put them to my small height, but my brothers would place them higher and higher very carefully so they wouldn't fall and break. We would get into a lot of trouble if we broke any bricks.

The kiln was heated by burning unrefined oil. The crude oil was dark and murky and burned with an acrid smell that filled the air for miles. It stank mightily for days while they baked the bricks. It got into our clothes and hair and seemed to stick to our skin. Even when it was finished, the world still reeked of the foul fires.

The kiln owner was always in a hurry to get his wares to the market and so would speed up the cooling process as much as he could. This usually meant more danger and pain for us. Instead of allowing the bricks to cool on their own, we simply poured water into the giant kilns to theoretically cool the bricks enough to handle.

I loved watching the giant clouds of steam hiss out of the holes in the kiln. When the steam had mostly all subsided, they would back their truck up to the entrance to the kiln, and my brothers and I would have to go into the "cooled-off" oven to retrieve the bricks.

We didn't have any protection for our hands, such as gloves or mittens, so we simply picked them up and took them from the kiln. Depending on their size, the bricks might weigh between two and five kilograms (five to ten pounds). They were also still very hot. The kiln itself was still stifling inside, and the fumes from the burning still lingered. We had to tie scarves around our mouths and noses, and it made my eyes water each time I entered. The top bricks were usually cooled off enough to handle fairly easily, but the deeper we got, the hotter it became. Many of the bricks were much too hot to handle for any amount of time, but we did it anyway. I remember my hands would be burnt and bleeding on the days we had to remove the bricks and load them to sell.

Each evening, we would return home, and my mother would fuss about me all over. She would see my dried, cut feet, my mud-coated body, and my blistered hands. She saw how tired I was in the morning and how beat my small body was. She would plead with my brother not to make me go anymore. There was a part of me that really wanted Bakir to agree with her and just let me sleep in the morning, but I also had this dream inside of me. The money we would earn would go to the family. If we didn't have enough money, as they all talked about, then I could do my part. Even at that young age, I still felt a great desire to contribute, and so I would get up every morning and go to work once again. Bakir was the brother who taught me to work. He believed that success came from hard labor, and even at that age, I could see that this might be my path to success. He taught me to work hard and to work smart. I saw that he worked as much with his brain as with his hands, and he was always careful and wise with his money. I tried to emulate that example. I will forever be grateful for the lessons he taught me.

Lost Innocence

In the United States, in general, people's lives are valued and protected. In particular, I realize how protected my son is. He was always monitored throughout his entire childhood. He also has no worries about family responsibilities, nor is he required to earn his keep. My childhood was not like this. Because of our cultural situation, we had very few chances to improve our financial position. As Kurds, we were ostracized from the rest of the country, and it felt like we could never get ahead. Therefore, any opportunity to work for money for our family was seen as a blessing, and we would take it regardless of how young we were. If you could work, then you did.

In the village, any news or opportunity always went through the two small teahouses or casinos, called *chayaxan* in Kurdish. Usually, they were open in the afternoon, and people enjoyed playing *gomond* and *dama* (it is a Kurdish game similar to checkers). The casinos sold sodas, muffins, and other juices. Both casinos were small and consisted of only one room. There were a few tables and plastic chairs to sit on as well. They were built as only one small community room. During the wintertime, when it was too cold to sit outside, there was never enough room or tables, so the men and boys would often have to stand to watch games being played because there was no place to sit. On the other hand, in the summertime, we could spread outside and sit on the porch area as well.

It was early summer; I believe the year was 1982. I was only eleven or twelve years old (remember, we rarely took notice of our birthdays or ages). People from the village gathered, enjoying their sodas, tea, and games. Suddenly, a small pickup truck stopped, and a couple of strangers jumped out of it. They started talking to the crowd about construction work they have in Gayra (Qayyarah), which was an Arab town about two hours away from our village. They said that they were hiring individuals who were interested in working for them. The salary was very low; however, most of the people who were unemployed in our village said that it was a great opportunity. I remember many of them wanted to go and work there.

The construction crew was building a military airport and housing for the Iraqi military officers outside the small town.

When I heard them discuss it, I asked my father if he would be okay with letting me go to work there during the summertime. He asked me if I knew anyone else who was going to work there. I named a few of my school friends, our neighbors, along with some of the individuals who were adults. One of my classmates, named Ghazi, who was a friend and neighbor, was going to be working there as well. I told my dad that he was going too. My father knew about Ghazi and his family's plight and so agreed to allow me to go, as much a support of Ghazi as for our family.

Ghazi was my age. He was one of the "orphans" of our village, though he was not really an orphan because he had a mother. At that time, if a family did not have a father, they were destitute. Women were not allowed to work outside the home, and so these families relied on the charity and generosity of their neighbors. Ghazi's mother was a widow, and he had one sister. They also had his grandmother living with them as well. His father had been killed during the 1960s–1970s Kurdish revolt against the Iraqi regime. By the Muslim and Kurdish definitions, he was considered an orphan. Because of their situation, many people in the village would be nice to them. It was so important in our society to have an adult male who could work and provide for the family. This opportunity then for Ghazi and his family was seen as a huge thing. Though we were still very young, it was a great honor for us, especially him, to be able to work and earn money for the family.

I think it was Friday when we packed our stuff and left the village. My mother gave me an old blanket and a small pillow, along with a couple of shirts and Kurdish pants. When I reflect back, I cannot remember if I took anything else or if there even was anything else to take.

Since the first day of school, when our home was ransacked by the Iraqi soldiers, I had never been at ease among the soldiers. There was a deep, abiding distrust I felt for them, and this new experience only heightened that discord. We were taken to the Qayyarah Military Airbase, sitting in the back of a small truck with my friends.

The moment we entered the gate, controlled by Iraqi intelligence officers, we were ordered to surrender our identification and leave it with them while we were working. This was our government-issued identification that allowed us movement within the country and, as such, was very important. It was also very cumbersome because it was nearly the size and shape of a school notebook. I had been warned by my parents to not lose my documents, but we were assured that they would be returned to us when we were finished, and we really had no choice in the matter. They took my identification along with those of all my companions and locked them up. We were never taken through that checkpoint again, so I never saw my ID again, either. Apparently, we actually didn't need those IDs.

We were taken to our rooms where we would be sleeping to drop off our meager bundles of supplies. The rooms were small and cramped. They stacked the rooms with beds, and there were about eight of us who all slept in the same small room. We had to get up early in the morning, at about 6:00 a.m., and we would work at the construction site until about 5:00 p.m. This working and sleeping arrangement was just a normal schedule for me. For many people, this may seem a terrible infraction of human rights to make children work; but for me and the other boys, to be allowed to earn some extra money was a godsend. Unfortunately, this opportunity turned into tragedy after only a week, and became a defining moment in my life.

It was summertime and hot. We had been working all that week on the construction job, and on this particular day, we were sweaty and restless. We were still boys, after all, and wanted to play. The River Zab, which flowed into the Tigris River, ran close to the area where we were staying; and we collectively decided to go swimming in the Great Zab or Upper Zab River. We all were from a small village and had never seen a big river like that. We didn't have swimming pools or places like that, so none of us was actually very good at swimming. Watching the fast current of water was both exciting and scary at the same time. The minute we walked into the river, I felt so scared and was not sure where and how to swim in such a big, fast river. The water was extremely cold, which was unexpected since it was summertime and so hot outside. It didn't take long, however, until we were all in the water, treading around and splashing like boys do. I am not a great swimmer, but I could at least keep my head above water.

Only one of my friends was a very good swimmer, but besides him, none of us were any good. Ghazi was just as bad as I was at swimming, but we were playing and didn't think about the dangers. He was swimming next to me when suddenly he started thrashing around and yelling for help. He had lost his footing in the cold, swift waters and couldn't keep his head above the surface. I quickly went to get close to him to try to help him, but instead of being able to help him, he grabbed onto me and started pulling me in as well. He was dragging me underwater, and I had to fight to get away from him because he was drowning me all the while we were being dragged farther and farther down the river into the deeper sections. I finally freed myself and splashed to relative safety, all the while calling out to the rest of the boys to see if anyone could help. My friend, the good swimmer, tried to catch him, but the water was so fast that he could not reach him to save him. I will never forget the last image I saw of my friend Ghazi. Both his hands were raised above the water, pleading for help as his head slowly sank below the rushing water. Soon he had disappeared in front of our eyes. We were all boys, and none of the adults came with us that day, so there was no one to help us. We felt hopeless in an area that was not part of our world. We couldn't go for help; we did not speak the language of the area. We all were Kurdish, and the town was all Arabic. We had only been there a week, and so we didn't know anybody with a boat or anything. Ghazi just disappeared. I never saw him alive again. Two weeks later, his body was recovered miles downstream from where he drowned.

This tragic event has never left me. The image of his hands has been seared into my memory. I cried for days, then weeks, and then months. Ghazi was in my mind day and night. I was so scared after what happened to Ghazi that I couldn't sleep well. I started sleeping next to my father instead of in the other room with my brothers. This went on for months. My life was changed forever. It was not just the fear of death that I felt. I also, for the first time, started to think about the state of other people. I felt so bad for his mother, sister, and grandmother. They had been so excited to have a young boy that was becoming a man. His life had meant that there was hope for them to escape poverty. This job had been a sign that they might have more in this life than what was left over from what others didn't want. He was the only son they had, but now he was gone, just as tragically and suddenly as the death of his father but just in a different way.

In a way, I started to link his death with that of his father and felt the injustice of both their deaths as the fault of the Iraqi oppression. He was gone, but I couldn't get over the finality of it. It was as if he had never existed in this world! Yet his memory was with us when we went to school. His memory wafted in the mosque and followed me even into my dreams and to the small shops in the town. It followed us to the field when we were playing soccer. Ghazi was no longer playing with us. There was just an empty spot where you couldn't kick the ball anymore. Ghazi's family lived close to our house. I started dreading walking past their home because every time I walked by their house, it felt like the tragedy had happened all over again. I could almost hear him yelling to me to come play soccer, and then I would remember him calling out to me for help and me actually pushing him away to save myself and then watching his hands fade slowly under the water.

The scar of this tragedy has always lived with me. As a child, I was scared and confused by death, and as I grew up, I still could not figure out how to deal with this inevitable fate. As a child, I was told that God gave us a gift, life, and he could decide to take our life back at any time. As a result, some live longer, and some live a very short time. As far as the Muslim religion was concerned, if a young child died, it was often interpreted that God loved them and wanted them back with him. In addition, we were taught that the world was full of sins and we all fell to temptation, so if someone died sooner, they were shortening their longevity of sin in this world, and they had a better chance to enter heaven sooner.

Even as a young child, however, the idea that death was just passing to a better place never really felt right to me. At that particular age, dealing with death was not an easy thing for me. My psychological state made me feel down all the time. I was not sure how to deal with the situation at all, and there was no counseling at all besides my family. However, time heals all wounds, as they say. As weeks and months passed, I started to forget and to slowly feel better. I believe having a big family was a huge help as well. I did not have to deal with loneliness as many kids did in our village or like the small family that was now missing their son, my friend Ghazi. I hoped that I would never have to go through such a loss again.

Direct Government Impact

In the early 1980s, my brother joined as a Peshmerga with the Kurdistan Social Party, which was very popular in our region. Being captured as a member of any political resistance party, such as the Peshmerga, in the late 1970s and early 1980s was almost like a death sentence. The Iraqi regime was robust militarily, and the Kurdish revolution had been recently crushed in 1975, so the trauma in the hearts and minds of the Kurdish people was still observable. Having Mohammed join the resistant armed Peshmerga group was hard for our family. It seemed impossible to hide anything from the government since spies were everywhere. Living in a small village full of bored and gossiping adults only added to the danger. As my father used to remind us often with the saying, "Even the wall has an ear."

Fortunately, he was never captured, which would have undoubtedly led to a swift execution. Even so, the pressure on him grew so hot that he decided to simply turn himself in. We were told that he had been seriously wounded in a battle. For his own health, the Peshmerga upper leadership allowed him to surrender to the Iraqi army, hoping for leniency and better health care than the Peshmerga could provide. After his healing, however, he was detained by the security apparatus, which usually meant that he would either disappear completely or be killed quickly. When my father heard the news, he was devastated. He tried to find out what was happening and why the government still detained Mohammed, but he could not find him, and no one knew where he was being held.

As a young boy, I remember the countless times my father left our village in search of news about his oldest son. He would take a taxi into the city (Hawler-Erbil) to seek him. He would knock on

39

the doors of every politician and government official. He did this fruitlessly for over six months to find his son. In most cases, he had to bribe the security guards, politicians, and handlers to even speak to someone in power about the fate of his son. He spent hundreds and thousands of Iraqi dinars to simply find someone who could tell him if Mohammed still lived. After many months, my father came back home from one of his long trips. My mother asked him, as always, if there was any news about Mohammed. He explained that he had finally found a judge in Kirkuk who seemed to have some knowledge and authority. My father explained that he had been so annoyed with the repeated visits and pleas that, in exasperation, he told my father, "If your son is alive, I will make sure he is not hanged. Now leave and go home."

There was nothing more we could do except wait for news. So for weeks, we went on with our lives, but I could tell that my father was constantly worried about Mohammed, and even though Mohammed was so much older than me and we had never been close, I was worried about him too. Finally, after more than a month of anticipation, we received a letter from the Iraqi government written in Arabic, saying Mohammed was being held in Abu Ghraib prison. It explained that he had been sentenced to twenty-five years in prison. The years of sentencing were inconsequential to us. The most important news was that he was still alive, and for our family, it was a liberation from all uncertainty about my brother. We celebrated that day, and it was as though a large weight had been taken off our lives. It was the happiest our family had been in a long time. I can still see the look of my father; you could see the joy seeping out of the worn lines of worry on his face.

Our village community received the happy news as well because good news spread as easily as bad news in such a small village as ours. Our community members came to visit our family, congratulating us and expressing their joy about the news. Now that we knew where he was, my parents wanted to see him. For a small boy, this seemed like an announcement for a family vacation. We were going to travel to the middle of Iraq near the capital. It was a five-hour drive, and it seemed so exciting, especially because of our joy and happiness, knowing he was still alive. My father rented a minibus to travel to Baghdad. As it turned out, my parents ended up making this trip monthly to visit Mohammed, and I always got to go with them. We woke up around 3:00 a.m. to leave. As I said, the trip was about four to five hours, and we would finally arrive around 7:00 or 7:30 a.m.

Years later, when the United States swept through Iraq, Abu Ghraib became internationally infamous. However, even before that time, stories of atrocities, torture, and murder were already well known about this prison. Its reputation was well deserved, and I remember the first time we entered Abu Ghraib; it felt like we had entered doomsday. I believe it was a Monday when we first arrived in Baghdad at the prison gate, so many people lined up to visit their loved ones. That was something I could never forget. The guards roughly separated and lined up the visiting people: males on one side and females on another. It was so scary to just be a visitor there. All the guards carried automatic rifles and constantly yelled orders at you. If you were in line and did not obey their rules quickly, you could get beaten by the guards with their hands or, more often, with the butt of their rifles. They treated the families of the prisoners as though they were guilty of the same crimes simply because they wanted to visit. My brother Bakir sternly commanded each of us children to quickly and quietly do exactly what the guards told us to do. It worked, I think mainly because we were often as scared of Bakir's punishments as though of the guards. We quietly stayed in our lanes and shuffled forward when it was our turn. These were Iraqi guards and, as such, had very little respect even for Arabic Iraqis, so for Kurdish Iraqis, it was even more dangerous. We really had to watch our behavior.

Even the cruel guards and the forbidding walls could not stave off our happiness. Finally, for the first time after almost two years, we saw my brother. He was still in his regular spirits. It was so like him to be confident and relaxed even in chains. I remember he was building some stuff that he had crafted in prison. We were amazed by what he had. I will never forget one gift he gave my older sister; it was a little purse, a little bag he had made, and he passed it over to her. She was so happy about that gift. Inside, the prison was chaotic during our visit. It was such a large complex that it would be very easy to get lost in it, which we did not want to do. People were everywhere, and obviously, my brother was not the only person who was handy at craftsmanship. Some of the prisoners were even selling their handcrafts. It felt like a minibazaar. We left that day with high spirits, thankful that he was alive and well, and hopeful that there would be a way to release him early.

My brother was in prison for about a year. All the while, we continued to visit him every month. Then, thankfully, we got some wonderful news. The Iraqi government, particularly Saddam Hussein, had given amnesty to all political prisoners. My brother was released in 1982.

Once again, I was thrust into situations that accentuated my ethnic differences. As a young Kurdish boy, I felt even more scared when we traveled to a strange land such as Baghdad. We had to be very cautious about our behaviors and what we said to other people during those trips. My sense of personal security was more deeply eroded. We were often subject to extreme scrutiny at the checkpoints because we all wore Kurdish clothes. I now realize that our obvious Kurdish heritage scared the Iraqi government security officials, who would have heard of the skirmishes and ongoing rebellion of the Kurdish Peshmerga. However, to a child, it just seemed like they were singling us out because we were different, so we had to do more extensive intrusive checks than other non-Kurdish citizens. During this event and my experience witnessing the Iraqi regime's brutal treatment of my people and my family, my sense of identity as a Kurdish was increasing, as was my disdain for the current regime in Iraq.

Selling Cigarettes

Growing up poor, we were always on the lookout for a chance to make some money. In a country run by secrecy and cruelty, it was easy to justify jumping into the black market. At that age and in those circumstances, I didn't have any qualms about doing it. The only issue I worried about was getting caught.

It was 1983, so I was about thirteen or fourteen years old. My older brother Bakir was always thinking about ways to support the family. One of his earlier schemes, before he started managing the family land, was to sell cigarettes. The Iraqi police claimed that selling cigarettes was illegal. The government controlled the legal market and didn't want competition. If the police saw someone selling them, they would detain that person, especially if it were a child, and confiscate all their merchandise. This was not because they were necessarily against cigarettes, nor were they working diligently to enforce the laws. No, the police did not care about other people selling cigarettes; they wanted to confiscate the cigarettes so that they could sell them themselves and make a good profit. Even with the risk, though, the possible profit was too much of a temptation to deny, so my brother was convinced that it would be good for him and our family. That was how I was pulled into the black-market operation as well.

He started this business of selling cigarettes from his relationship with two brothers, their names Khidir and Shuker (Khidir was my brother's age and his best friend). They were from our village, Peerdawood. Those three organized the operation but then brought me and another one of their brothers, Lateef, who was a few years older than me, into their ploy.

I was even caught at one point. I was out selling on the streets in a dark area of the community bazaar. When we sold them, we would walk quietly between shoppers and then hold out a handful of cigarettes to people and ask them quietly if they wanted to buy some cigarettes. We had to constantly watch our backs to see if there were any military personnel or police around. At one point, I was intently engaged in a potential sale when suddenly gruff hands seized me from behind. I was so scared. The police officer slapped me across the face, stole all the cigarettes that I was carrying, trying to sell (I had hidden the rest in case I was caught), gripped my arm, and dragged me off to jail. Years later, when I was in America, I watched old Western movies and realized that the jail I was put into looked like it could have been used as a set for an American cowboy film.

I was locked up in jail and threatened with bodily harm if I made a move or tried to shout. I was so scared. I kept thinking about visiting my brother in Abu Ghraib, and now my poor mother and father would have to come to visit another one of their poor children in prison. I was convinced that I was going to be sent far away and maybe spend years in detention. Fortunately, my brother showed up a few hours after being caught and got me out. I have no idea how he convinced the guards to let me go, but I was so relieved to be out of that place.

This run-in with the law didn't deter our business, though. As so often happens in family businesses, the older ones do the organizing, and the younger ones get stuck with the work and travel. Our family-owned the transportation, our motorcycle, and I already knew how to ride it, so I was often the driver that had to do pickups and deliveries. One day, my brother asked me to take Lateef and ride to another town to bring a box of cigarettes for them to sell. Lateef was older than me by a year or two, and besides that, he was very tall. Nonetheless, I knew how to drive, and it was our family's vehicle. So I started the motorcycle and jumped on it, and Lateef rode in the back, holding onto me.

My older brother Bakir on his Motorcycle

On our way to our destination, close to a small town called Kuran, there was a traffic light at an intersection. I maneuvered the bike slowly between a couple of cars to get to the front of the cue. One of them was an old Russian car called a Lada. It was being used as a taxi; I will never forget that car. As we were winding between all the cars, my elbow bumped into the side of that taxi. I thought nothing of it besides how it stung my elbow, and I continued forward without a backward glance.

Even though nothing had happened to the car, the taxi driver leaned out of his window and shouted at us to stop. I yelled back over my shoulder, "Why? Nothing happened to your car. My elbow hurts, but your car is fine." I was shouting back at him as the light turned green, and we were moving again on the road. He started yelling and swearing at us, "I say, stop, *father dog*," which is a very vulgar insult. I did not care what he was saying, but I was a little scared of what he would do to us, so I started driving faster.

The taxi driver must have swerved recklessly through the cars in front of him, because suddenly he was right behind us. He started laying on his horn and cussing us while trying to get us to stop. Lateef shouted at me to just stop, but I was too scared of this crazy taxi driver. I started driving blindly through the town while he doggedly chased us everywhere. I was still a fairly new driver. I was short and very young. The road was wet and muddy, and there were pools of standing water everywhere. I tried so hard to lose this taxi, but I just couldn't shake him. All the while, Lateef was pleading with me to just pull over. Unfortunately, the taxi driver obviously knew this area much better than I did, and soon we were running out of turns to get away. Eventually, I turned onto a small side road and discovered that it was a dead end into an alley. We could not run any longer.

When I stopped and faced the car, the taxi driver stopped too. He got out of his car, but instead of coming straight to us, he walked to the back of his car and opened his trunk. I wasn't sure what he was doing, and it made me even more nervous. When he closed the trunk, he was carrying a huge iron stick, probably a tire iron of some sort. Now that he was armed, he started moving toward us. I started shaking so badly with fear. He was an angry adult coming toward us with a large metal rod. I just knew that he was going to kill us both and leave our poor crumpled bodies right there in the alleyway. I was still on my motorcycle, not sure if I should try to gun it and get past him or maybe talk myself out of this predicament. While I hesitated, Lateef stepped off the back of the seat. I knew I couldn't leave him, so I put my motorcycle on break and waited to see what the man was going to do to me. I felt bad that I had gotten Lateef, who was older and bigger than me, into this predicament and hoped that maybe the man would only get mad at me and leave Lateef alone, who was obviously not at fault and probably much more responsible than that short little boy.

To my surprise and horror, the taxi driver went straight toward Lateef. He brandished the iron bar and started waving it around like he was about to hit him. All the time, he was shouting insults calling him, "Sagi Sagbab, why do not stop!" Lateef and I were so surprised. Dumbfoundedly, he whined, "Why are you calling me names? I was not driving. He was the driver, and I asked him to stop."

"He is only a kid. You are older. You should have stopped him."

Lateef tried again, "But I told him, and he did not want to stop."

At this moment, I saw my opportunity. I stepped between both of these men who were arguing and petitioned the taxi driver to please not hit Lateef. I became the arbitrator in the fight, even though it was basically my fault. I stood between them, ensuring that Lateef didn't get hurt, and also as a distraction for the taxi driver.

I told the taxi driver, "Please stop. Do not hurt him."

Then he looked at me and said, "Why didn't you stop?"

I hung my head in a dejected humble stance and said, "I'm sorry, but we are in a hurry to get some stuff for our brothers and did not want to be late."

He could see that we were both young; and the minute I mentioned a duty to my brothers, he stopped, took a deep breath, and pointed out of the alley, "Just go, please, and do not do that ever again."

While we were racing out of that alley street, I said, half to myself, "Why would I do that ever again!"

Lightning Strikes Twice

My son, Ari, is an only child. That was not planned, but it is just what happened. He will never have a brother or sister to confide in. He also doesn't have to compete with anyone. He gets all the attention of both his mother and me. He has his own room, his own toys, his own clothes. And he is perfectly happy. My own situation was so different. I shared everything I had with my brothers. We slept all together, all ten of us, in two small rooms; we ate together, played together, fought together. I didn't have many toys, but they were all just family toys. I also had so many people I could talk to and tell secrets too. I sometimes feel bad that Ari will never have that opportunity.

Unfortunately, in such a poor agricultural community, the dangers are not just present for boys; any person is susceptible to death at any moment. Losing Ghazi was the first experience that I had had with death. However, as I grew older, I realized how much mourning I would have to wade through.

Our village was in the countryside, which was very open and flat. The region is historically known as Shamamk and Mirkya. The land is prominent for its fertility when it comes to agriculture. When we look back through history, our region is at the top of the Fertile Crescent, the cradle of civilization as it were. Reading the history of the region, one will realize how important agriculture has been in this region. The earliest records of the first invention of agriculture started in the region thousands of years ago. Kurds have always depended on the land and used it as the main survival tool throughout their history.

Our region, however, is not always very wet. In fact, it gets hot and dry, especially during the summer. We didn't have great rivers that ran through our land; those were miles away. As a result, water was sacred in the area. Consequently, wells and underground canals have been the main source of water for this particular area. New wells were always constantly being dug to find more water sources.

I was about twelve years old when my brother Bakir came back from the military and started our new family farming business. We all worked together to help the business to ensure success and productivity to support our family. In a couple of years, the business showed great success. My brother built another room next to the main house for guests. We had enough land to extend and build another room. Our life started getting much better financially.

(From Left my older brother Bakir, Salah and Abdulkhaliq) working in the farm

My brother bought a small truck to transfer his vegetables to sell in the market. In addition, he got married just a few months later. Our farm business was doing well. My brother was fully in charge. He was managing the business solely. I would say he was a very smart man and a good business manager. He had such great interpersonal skills; people would trust him instantly once he started a conversation with them. I loved his way of interacting with different types of people to be successful in his business transactions. However, his way of interacting with us as brothers and sisters was a different story. He was always full of restrictions and requirements. Without his permission, nothing was permitted, period! Even my father would not interfere in the decisions he would make regarding the business and then sometimes in our family responsibilities as well. My father came to trust him fully with the daily decisions he made in our family affairs.

My life became very stressful and busy. I now had a new boss, and he was so strict. If it wasn't for my older sister Gulizar, I might have gone crazy. She was my confidant, my laughter, my refuge from the daily tolls of life. My sister and I were so comfortable together. It wasn't that we had deep, powerful conversations. We could just be ourselves around each other. It was always so easy to talk to her, and we had good discussions, nothing special, just sister-and-brother talk.

Gulizar was two years older than me. She was my older sister, so I respected her a lot. However, it was different from the relationship I had with my older brothers. They told me what to do, and I had to do it (even if I really didn't want to). Gulizar was my best friend. We joked around together, we laughed a lot together, and we even cried together, especially after my friend Ghazi died. She was so compassionate and understanding.

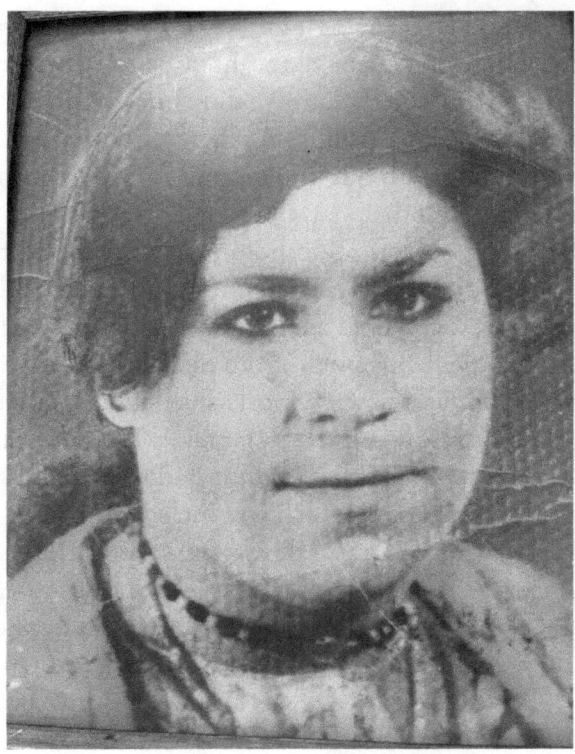

My sister, Gulizer

She introduced me to many things in the world. Like most young boys, I didn't really think about how I looked, what I wore, or how girls would think about me. Sometimes, Gulizar would critique my choice of clothes for school. Though she didn't go to school, she still wanted me to look good. When I went out with my friends, she would also make suggestions on how to look good. On many different occasions, she would stop me before I could run out the door to just comb my hair. She then joked, "You look good, and girls will like you." I would laugh back. "No, they won't. You just say that because you are my sister."

We talked about everything with each other, and we had a lot of time to talk. Our brother made us work very hard, but it wasn't so bad because I could work next to my sister. Since it was summertime, we would go to the farm every day and work next to each other in the field all day. We talked and told secrets to each other. We would make jokes a lot and laugh and laugh. My older brother would often scold us for talking too much. He wanted us to just work and not talk. We tried to work quietly, but we didn't heed him for very long, and we then went back to talking. At the end of the day, we would ride back to our home with our donkey and cart together as well. We were very close to each other.

One day, my sister left to go home earlier than me to help my mother prepare dinner. Finally, after sunset, my other siblings and I headed home to eat together as a family. We were tired and walked in the gate, expecting delicious smells from our dinner waiting. Instead, when we arrived home, I saw everyone shocked and crying as well. Everything is a blur in my mind at this point. I am not sure whom I asked, but someone told me that Gulizar had been seriously burnt.

To cook, we had a stove which was fueled with an oil called *ple-miz* (in Kurdish, it is called *nafit*). It was similar to kerosene, so it was very flammable. We cooked with it every day, so we rarely thought of how dangerous it was to light the fuel. However, when Gulizar was preparing hot water for dinner, somehow, she caught fire when she tried to light the stove. My sister-in-law told me that my older brother Bakir had taken her to the hospital, and my mother had also gone with them. This happened just minutes before we arrived home. I anxiously asked how bad it was, but they said they didn't know. They were so solemn; I feared the worst.

My sister was in the burn unit in the Erbil hospital for a couple of weeks. Her burning was very severe. I got to visit her once. She was not able to talk that much. I asked her how she was doing. She barely whispered with her typical positive attitude, "Okay." Her body was all covered in bandages. She closed her eyes and fell asleep. That was the last time I would see her alive. I still remember the horrific scene of her suffering as a result of burning. I could not believe how fast this incident took place, nor will I forget how fast she passed out of my life.

After Gulizar passed away, my life was upside down. I was completely devastated. The death of my sister twisted my soul so badly and left me sleepless again. Weeks dragged into months, and months turned into years. It affected so many things in my daily life. I dreamed about her often, and in my *dreams*, we talked and laughed, but I would wake up from my dream and realize it was only a dream; I fell into an even deeper depression. Others around me noticed this, especially my mother.

My mother has always been a strong woman. After we started our farming business, she was both a full-time mother and a full-time farmer in the field. We all helped, but I admired her effort and hardworking skills that no one in the family could compete with. I still remember her out in the fields in the middle of summer during the fasting month of Ramadan. She refused to eat or drink, as was expected in Islam, but she never slackened her hand. No matter what time of the day it was, her hands were busy, and her feet never stopped. She always worked from before I woke in the morning until sunset. She was very stoic and never complained; she was always kind, though, and would have good conversations with us and, most importantly, was always available to meet our needs when we asked. After my sister passed away, I remember how devastated she was, and it was especially poignant because of how positive she usually acted.

Even through her grief, though, she still reached out to give comfort. As she watched me and could see what I was going through, she quietly sat, counseled me, and explained that such a tragic event could happen to anyone and at any time in life. She would sit with me for a long time and try to get me to stop crying. I knew she was suffering more than anyone in our family, though, because sometimes she would just start crying. In my day, it was common that the parents were expected to hold their emotions in and not lose control, so my father would try to calm her, but it rarely worked. She would not let even her grief stop, though, and she continued to be the mother even through her tears. She always reached out to try to comfort me especially.

My father comforted me in a different way. In our culture, men should show strength even in events like the death of their own daughter or son, and they must never show any sign of weakness. I could see and feel the pain he was going through, but he always used to say, "Alhamdulillah" (which means, "Thank you, God"). I never saw him cry, not once. Since he was the head of the family, his duty was to ensure the rest of the family and my siblings were well and psychologically not affected by such a tragic event. He was not unkind, though, and did his best to offer comfort to his small children. I would often put my head down on his lap. Then he would rest his hand on my head and offer comfort by stroking my hair. It offered some comfort for a few minutes, but later on, I would see something that reminded me of her and again find myself in agony and pain. I remember how my father comforted even my mother. When she started crying, he would say, "Khadij, please say, 'Alhamdulillah.' Praise your God. You still have your other children."

The innocence of my youth was beaten, cracked, and then shattered by these three major events. What had begun as a very simple life—with a secure home, good friends, and a complete, loving family—was now all in disarray. I had no sense of security from the government controlling our poor village and people. My friend's life had been taken, and then it was followed so quickly by my sister's life. I was not sure if I would ever feel at peace again. This shattering of my innocence pushed me to learn more about the world, history, life, and my culture. I was so empty; I felt I needed something to fill me up. I didn't know what, if anything, would ever fill that void.

Education

As a child, I didn't prize education. Instead, I looked to my brother Bakir, who taught me that work gives a man his place in the world. "Work is an honor, no matter what job you hold." He beat that message into me over and over. As a man, we were responsible for providing for our family. This was the key message: a man must support his family. The actual work didn't matter. A demanding job should never discourage you, no matter where you work—teacher, construction, or farmworker. All work is hard; it is part of life. Whenever I reflect on my past—working in the field, making bricks, doing construction for the military—I am not sure how my little body even handled such hard work. I'm not sure how I survived in the sweltering summer heat. I often compare my childhood to all the jobs I have held in the United States and especially the kind of work I do now. It amazes me that I did not even complain then. However, sometimes in the United States, I complain to my family and friends, "I am tired. It is so hard sitting all day on a chair. The air conditioning is too cold, the copy machine is not working, and my boss wants me to stay an extra half hour for a meeting." I have forgotten the kind of jobs and work I did as a child in Kurdistan. If I had been in any industrialized country, my family could have faced criminal charges for child labor laws.

As I grew older, though, I started to realize that there was more to life than just work. While Bakir taught me to work, my other older brother Burhan taught me the love of study. He was the scholar of the family. He was always reading and studying. He knew so many things about everything. My mother and father were humble people. They had always lived on the land and simply accepted things as they were. Neither of them could read, and I think this really affected my brother. He wanted to know everything. Even before that hunger was awake inside my own mind, I could see his brain contorted by the conflicting messages he got from his learning.

My brother Burhan

When he wasn't working, it seemed that Burhan always had a book in his hand. He loved to read. Before starting school, I would watch him. I longed to figure out what he was doing while staring at the pages. There were no children's books in our home, and I had never been read to as a child. The only book we had in our home was the Qu'ran, which my father clung to in times of distress or confusion. He believed that just holding the holy writ would protect and inspire him, and maybe it did sometimes.

He was not an ignorant man; he just never got a formal education, though he always valued education. He wanted me to value it as well. When I was about nine or ten years old, my father asked me, when I came home from school, if I could write his name down. I said, "Yes, Dad, sure I can." I wrote his name, showed him his name, and said, "Here it is, Dad. This is your name." My father replied, "I'm sorry, my son, I can't read this. I just wanted to see if you were able to write my name." He paused for a moment for an idea to sink in. Then he continued, "You are too young to see, but when it comes to reading and writing, I am a blind person. I wish I had the ability to read and write." He continued, "Education is a precious thing, son, and hold on to it. If I ever could read, I would read this valuable book." (He was pointing his finger to the Qu'ran on the shelf). As I grew, he occasionally asked me to read it for him out loud, which was difficult for a young child, but I would usually try my best...if I couldn't come up with a decent childish excuse.

Chapter 2

Teenage Years

Kurdistan

It is in the very nature of adolescence to rebel. There is some aspect of humanity that drives a teenager to fight against the bounds that society has proscribed. Revolutions have always used the impetuous nature of youth to fuel their anger and supply their forces. Kurdistani youth are no different. Though from my perspective, they have a much stronger justification than many of the rebellious youth I see in my neighborhood.

Map of Kurdistan

Though young children see the injustices thrust upon them (doing dishes, cleaning their room, being sent to bed early, and not being able to play video games), they have no power or will to resist the authority which compels them to submit. As they grow, however, that meek submission falls away, and they have a keen desire to flex their growing muscles of independence.

As a child, I was not oppressed by my family. My mother and father were loving and permissive. I did not have a curfew, nor was I forced to do my homework. I rarely even had to bathe, so as I approached those turbulent teenage years, I found another avenue of oppression that I could butt my head against—the government.

The events of my childhood, our poverty, government disdain and oppression, and the persecution of Kurds finally all swelled up in my mind and created a persistent questioning of the world I found myself in. I started studying the history of my country, people, and

Kurdistan. I wanted to know why I was so different and why being different was such a disadvantage to me and my family.

Besides the direct oppression by the Iraqi military, such as the cruel aggression on our village on my first day of school, there were many times when I brushed up against the powerful force of history that pervaded that land that had been fought over for millennia.

Finding Silver Coin

As I said, I was becoming fascinated by the history of the Middle East region, and Kurdistan, in particular. The more I read about Kurdish history, the more I realized how oppressed we have been by those who occupied our land and controlled our lives in the past and present. How these rulers systematically oppressed Kurdish people in every aspect of life. They deprived us of the simplest and most basic human rights, such as reading and writing in our mother tongue. As a result, we never have had the luxury of recording our history for centuries. Kurdish people started practicing reading and writing vastly in their language in the late nineteenth century.

the old coin that found by Dr. Bewar's mother

When the Muslim rulers took over and occupied Kurdistan, many Kurdish scholars and intellectuals arose, although almost all of them were writing in Arabic and only occasionally in other languages. Their main topics were about Islam, but they also included some history. Those Kurdish writers and scholars served the interest of the Muslim faith and Arab or Persian language rather than serving their own. The main reason for that was the education system, mostly either in Arabic, Turkish, or Persian. There was no schooling or Madrasa available in the Kurdish language. In his book *Picking Flowers along the Way*, Mr. Neshrwan Mustafa, one of the leading Kurdish scholars and political leaders, talks about some of the well-known Kurdish writers Ibin Khulakan and Jaban al-Kurdi. All their books were written in Arabic. Yet these scholars were Kurdish born in Kurdistan. Another famous Kurdish writer, Sharafkhxani Badlisi (1543–1603), wrote one of the first Kurdish history books *Sharafnama*, but it was written in Persian. So it was shameful and insulting that the only way I could read Kurdish history was in a foreign language and from an outside culture because most of them have been written by others who were not Kurdish. As a result, it is hard to believe all the historical events that have been recorded were not somehow distorted. These writers and scholars are only an example of the completely tragic history of our nation.

We clearly see and feel how these empires or rulers—such as the Arab, Persian, and Turkish rulers—were purposefully undermining the Kurdish nation's role in building the ancient civilizations and the new civilization in the Middle East. When you read the history of the region, no one talks about the Kurdish people. All other nations want to take credit for the old civilizations and ignore those who lived there. When you look at Mesopotamia's early culture and read about it, it was developed in the heart of Kurdistan. But, unfortunately, no one throughout any history books ever mentioned the name of the Kurdish people. If they do, very rarely. In his book, Mr. Nesherwan says Mesopotamia's civilization has always been closer to the Kurdish people geographically than any other nation in its surrounding, such as Arabs, Turks, or Persian. Nevertheless, Kurdish culture is never mentioned throughout history. An event happened in those teenage years that bears testimony to the longstanding history of Kurdistan and how it has existed as the fertile crescent of empires for thousands of years. This story is only one piece of evidence of the historical treasure of Kurdish land and Kurdistan.

I remember a story from my youth, and it's about my family. The land surrounding most of the villages near Erbil was divided into farmland, like our plot. The region is mostly flat, but there are many small hills that dot the entire countryside. On one such hill, my brother had decided to try to flatten it to have more land to grow his crop. That piece of land was tough to use because irrigation and watering that hill were very hard. He hired someone from our village to do that for him. It was one of the few people who owned a bulldozer at the time. He started flattening the hill as others came to watch, fascinated, as he pushed dirt around and flattened down the small hill.

As the dirt was dug up and pushed around, my mother bent down and picked something shiny off the ground. She furtively called my dad and brother over to her out of earshot of the bulldozing worker. In her hand, she held out a small handful of silver coins. Maybe about five to six coins. I remember my mother whispering in my brother's and father's ears. She told them she had found some silver coins under the soil. They had been buried in a kind of sack, which deteriorated as she picked it up. They quickly decided to keep the coins secret because if the government found out that they had found such historical artifacts, they would take the coins and the land. That story, as with most secrets, was kept as best it could. I actually got to see one of the coins. As I have explained before, I studied history, and I thought I recognized the ancient markings. The coins were silver, and I believe they belonged to the *Seleucid* era.

Like all the other families in the village, we were not rich. My parents saw this find as a blessing from heaven. They excitedly but secretly took these few coins to the city of Erbil and showed them to a goldsmith they trusted. The man offered them a nominal, insignificant amount of money for these priceless artifacts. Since they wanted the money and cared nothing about history (from my perspective), they sold the small treasure for only a few dinars. It only paid for a few extra basic necessities, such as food or clothing. To me, that piece of silver was worth much more than ten or twenty dinars at the time.

It was part of our Kurdish history; it should have never been given away that easily or sold to anyone. But it was done. Luckily, I was able to convince my parents to give me and still have it.

Even as a young teenager, I cared a lot for the heritage of my people, but even if I had spoken up, no one would have cared about my opinion. Who would listen to a naive inexperienced young boy like me?

The coins reminded me that we Kurds lived on land that was much older than just our family's time. In school, we had learned about ancient civilizations, and suddenly, those ancient histories became real to me. Someone had buried their money right on this piece of land, maybe a thousand or two thousand years ago. I had no way of knowing how long, but the mystery awoke in me a sense of fascination with the past.

Forbidden Knowledge

It was during this time that I became a cultural historian. I started reading everything I could about Iraq, Kurdistan, the Asian Empires, and religions. I wanted to know and understand. Much of the information was accessible, though highly censored, in my school and in the libraries in Erbil.

Burhan, my older brother, had finally finished secondary school and was now starting college. He loved it and would bring his books and interests home with him. I wasn't supposed to, but I would sneak his books when he wasn't aware. I especially liked the histories and the poetry. The histories were much more complete than what I had access to at our village school, and I started to see patterns and forces I hadn't known about before. The poetry, on the other hand, sang to me as nothing else had. It seemed to awaken in me a longing for a past that never existed and a future that could never arrive. I would spend long hours poring over the prose. I even shed tears at times while considering the losses and pain that the words evoked.

I had to have more—I had to know more. Burhan started to bring home material that was not in the school curriculum. In fact, because he was at a school in Erbil, the unofficial capital of Kurdistan (a nation that only existed in the minds and hearts of a conquered people), he found access to many contraband books. These he also brought home, and they were much more helpful in fueling my curiosity and seditious attitude than the dry censored history books.

The books themselves were fairly tame. They did not call for war or rebellion. They simply attempted to give an accurate portrayal of Kurdistan's history, albeit from a Kurdish perspective. As I read about its history, it became my history. The men and women who fought, who died, and who were conquered and oppressed were my brothers and sisters, uncles, aunts, mothers, and fathers. I felt a poignant sense of nationality and anger.

This memoir is not a history of Kurdistan or the Kurdish people. However, in order to understand my indignation and justification for my future actions, I feel it is necessary for you to understand what I came to know. I didn't learn this as I present it here. It was pieced together over many years, some of which I only learned after coming to America. Nonetheless, it makes more sense in chronological order.

Kurdistan is the traditional land of the Kurdish people. The history of the Kurdish people goes back to the Assyrian and Babylonian eras stretching more than three thousand years ago (it was one of these that I imagined the coins we found belonged to). It was during the Ottoman Empire that the name Kurdistan was initially used to call the region inhabited by the Kurdish people. There are many documents of those empires that show on maps, an area called Kurdistan. As you may know, the idea of statehood or a recognized country is a modern conception. Countries and states simply existed only as long as they could defend against another city-state or nation. In the West and throughout Europe, the ideas of countries and borders were prevalent throughout the age of reason but not so in much of the rest of the world. In particular, in the Middle East, the rise of nations only took place after World War I. Before this, the lands were simply parts of conquering empires. The Kurds did have Imarat (referring to concepts similar to a subjective state) under both the Ottoman Empire and Iranian Safavid Dynasty, similar to confederate states such as Baban, Botan, Soran, Ardalan, etc.

Though always coveted and often conquered, Kurdistan as a land was always kept intact. However, the fertile land finally was split as empires all wanted a piece of its bounty. The first division of Kurdistan started in the early 1500s. between the Ottoman Empire and the Safavid Dynasty of Iran during the Chaldiran Battle. After long years of fighting between these two superpowers, often battling each other on the land of the Kurdish people, Sultan Salim defeated the Ismail Shah. This victory was accomplished with the help of some of the Kurdish tribes who helped Sultan Salim based on an agreement between the Sultan and some of the Kurdish chiefs. However, this alignment divided the people and eventually doomed their prospect for self-government for hundreds of years.

After World War I, the Ottoman Empire collapsed; and the land of the Kurdish people (Kutherdistan) was divided among four countries, Syria, Turkey, Iran, and Iraq. The biggest section, which currently has a population of about twenty million, is part of the modern Republic of Turkey. The second-largest portion of Kurdistan went to Iran, third was Iraq (which is where I was born), and Syria got the smallest part of Kurdistan. Though the land was highly coveted and welcomed, the Kurdish people were not welcomed into the national structure in any part of these countries, and their rights were quickly subverted. In fact, most of these countries tried to wipe out the idea of Kurdish heritage altogether. Kurds in Turkey were renamed Mountain Turks, and their mother language was forbidden until the 1990s. Kurds in Syria were not even given Syrian citizenship. In Iran, similar cultural and political oppression was applied, and you already know how Kurds were treated in Iraq from my own childhood accounts. As a result of these injustices, Kurds throughout the twentieth century had to continually fight for their basic rights of survival. Unfortunately, that fighting still continues.

Kurdistan of Iraq (which is where I was born) was forcefully annexed to the new modern country of Iraq by Britain. The new Iraq was initially set up as a kingdom ruled by King Faysal, who ruled the nation under a feudal system of governance. The Kurds of Iraq, already an ethnic minority with few rights and few decisions in their futures, were now forced to become Iraqi citizens under feudal law, making them little more than serfs to their Iraqi Lords or sheiks, as they were called. In Kurdistan, there was very little spent on infrastructure in developing their villages, and the people were kept fairly oppressed. Historically, most of the land was always owned by *aghas* and *sheiks*, noble titles similar to a duke or lord. This continued under that regime as well. The peasant Kurds worked the land they had traditionally worked for years yet still no longer owned.

There was some change and possibility for hope, however, after World War II. In 1958, a man named Kassam overthrew the monarchy and abolished the feudal system throughout Iraq. His land reform measures included giving land to the head of each family that worked it. My family was one of the lucky ones who received land from the government. However, the reforms and hopes for a more benevolent rule were dashed. In 1963, Kassam was captured in a military coup by Ba-athists when he was only forty-eight. He was executed in the capital city, Baghdad, by the new ruling party—the Ba'ath regime. The Ba'ath Party took control with a young commander who slowly consolidated his power until he was made president and ruled as dictator of Iraq. His name was Saddam Hussein.

The Fall of the Monarchy

For my own family, our fortunes started with the Kassim regime in 1958, which was a turning point by any standard on the cultural and economic prosperity of our land. During Kassim's short reign, most lower-class people were happy about the changes. Iraq was now the Republic of Iraq, and it seemed that they were entering the twentieth century with the rest of the world. Abdul Karim Kassem, also spelled Abd al-Karīm Qāsim, was the president, and the government system shifted for many Iraqis and Kurds. The new government system was much better for poor people and cultural minorities. Despite the fact that this revolt was considered to have been carried out by a group of Pan-Arabs, Kassem was determined to solve internal issues as well as the internal struggles he was confronting. One of his solutions for the poverty of many Iraqis was to distribute land to the previous peasant class. The system of feudalism had been in place since the Ottoman Empire ruled Iraq. Even after Iraq was born as a country under British colonization, it still continued. In Iraq, 80 percent of the land was owned by less than 2 percent of the population, and Kurdistan's land was mostly owned by agha (dukes) or sheiks.

This major inequity led to the new government starting a land reform program, which was called the Agrarian Reform Law. The new regime took most of the lands from the *aghas* (dukes) and distributed it to the people who lived in the rural areas to cultivate wheat and barley. According to many scholars whom I read about as a youth, this law benefited Iraq and its people in the process of social and economic development. Every head of the household who lived in the rural areas was given about sixty acres of land to support their own family. Finally, the people who lived on the land owned it and could use it to grow or raise their own food and products to sell. They were no longer under the oppression of feudalism. Unfortunately, all did not go well between the Kurds and Iraqis. The New Iraqi president had attempted to solve the land and governance issue with the Kurdish revolutionists, but they were unsatisfied and wanted their own self-governance, which Kassem was not willing to offer. After three years of discussions and meetings, negotiations broke down. As a result, Kurdistan of Iraq announced an armed struggle against the Iraqi regime. This Kurdish revolution was led by a famous Kurdish leader, Mustafa Barzani, who played a much larger role in my own life later on. The Kurdish revolution gained momentum from 1960 to 1970 with the support of the *shah* of Iran. However, in 1970, Barzani entered into negotiations with the Iraqi government. For a brief moment, it seemed that the Kurds would finally be recognized. However, there was a political upheaval, and the Ba'ath Party overthrew Abdulkarim's regime, and the hopes of a Kurdish autonomy were dashed. Ahmed Hassan Bakir became the president, with Saddam Hussein as his vice president. Saddam was really the major player even though he was only the VP at the time. His leadership and political skills convinced Iran to stop its support of the Kurdish revolution, and as a result, the revolution soon collapsed in 1975.

When Saddam Hussein formally took power in 1979, the life of the Kurdish people worsened under his regime. During his reign, the neglected feeling of the government toward the Kurds was replaced with animosity. Most of the Kurdish people now felt unsafe even in their own villages and homes, particularly because the security apparatus and government intelligence agencies were everywhere. No matter where you lived, no one felt safe talking about the regime of Saddam himself. It goes without saying then that it was rare to even criticize him or the government, even within your own family circles. Over the years, I came to better understand what my father had told me long before when my brother had joined the Peshmerga that "even the wall has an ear."

Despite the oppression and regime changes, my grandfather and father were determined to make the most of their newfound property rights. They were, by nature, industrious, motivated, and smart. Now that he had land, my grandfather was able to procure sheep, goats, and other livestock. He used his money wisely and soon was doing very well. My father inherited a portion of the land (it was divided between him and his brothers) and continued the business. He did well for himself and our family. Based on this money management and thriving business, we had comfortable living conditions compared to many in our small village. Many people in the village considered my father to be financially in a better position. In fact, because my father owned livestock, he was considered wealthy at that time. I remember we even had a hired shepherd named Sabeer, who took care of our sheep and goats. I was very young and barely remember that much about Sabeer. In the 1970s, when I was very young, my father hired him as our shepherd, God bless his heart. He was very funny and a hard worker. My parents and the rest of the family did not treat him differently from any of us. He would eat with us and sleep in our home with us as well. He was part of our family. He stayed as long as we owned livestock.

When I was about ten, I believe, my father sold all the sheep he had, and I was so happy about that transaction because I felt like I was always helping, and I hated to take care of any kind of livestock. Sabeer left, as well, when we no longer owned sheep. My father told us in consolation that Sabeer was now married and had a family of his own. I never saw him again, and only years later, my brother told me that Sabeer had passed away. Meanwhile, we still kept some animals for our home of course; we still had a couple of goats, some chickens, turkeys, and other poultry—for the family only, though.

We had lived my whole childhood on the money and food from the livestock and also the seasonally harvested grain: wheat and barley. It was always a modest living. Though we were comfortable, we really still had very little. Later on, our village got electricity but still no running water or gas. As I said, we had only a small two-room mud home with dirt floors. It wasn't until years later as a teenager that things started to change really. When my older brother Bakir took over, it changed our fortunes for a time. He started a new business using our land, growing tomatoes, eggplants, cucumbers, turnips, red beets, etc.

Secret Actions

As I was entering those critical adolescent years, living under such oppressive conditions and seeing how Saddam's regime was persecuting and mistreating the Kurdish people, along with how he dealt with any who opposed him, you can well see how my interests were piqued in history and politics. My interest drew me especially to the Kurdish resistance and history of the Kurdish nation. Following the death and mourning of my friend and especially my sister, learning about the long-standing abuses of my people, my brother's incarceration, and the new atrocities carried out by the regime only added more stress to my previously simple life. It seemed to kindle a fire inside me, but instead of trying to extinguish the flame, I started to seek out more fuel to increase my passion. I started watching and listening to political news and forbidden materials about the Iraqi government. I knew, even as I was collecting it, that this contraband information could lead to persecution and imprisonment for me and my family, but my desire to know the truth was too strong.

Dr. Kamal Bewar, Teenage 1983

In 1983, when I was about fourteen, after my older brother Mohammed had been released from prison, instead of staying safe and trying to lead a normal life with his wife and children, he went directly back to the rebellion as a Peshmerga. This time, he joined the Kurdish Communist Party, in Kurdish, Heezby Shu'y (this was different from the organization that I would eventually join: the PUK). They used Mohammed for intelligence gathering, so he was always in the city of Erbil, hiding and doing clandestine activities. I was still young and fairly inconspicuous, so I was the perfect age to support his rebellious acts. He would hide during the day and come out at night to do his activities against the government with his group. He continued doing them for some time even though it seemed they were constantly being thwarted and his missions (and, therefore, mine) became increasingly dangerous. He found out later that his leader was selling them out, and my brother was only protected because he never really trusted anyone in the first place.

I idolized my brother so much that I would follow him at night and help him. He would give me notes to deliver secretly, or he would send me on small reconnaissance missions. My mother and father still lived in the Peerdawood Village at that time, so this happened when I went to stay at my aunt's house. I did not tell my family about this. Usually, I just told them I was with my cousin Aziz or Mohammed. My aunt (Raheema) hated it when my brother would take me out in the middle of the night, but since it was Mohammed, he could get away with whatever he wanted. I can remember silently walking the streets in the dead of night. He was so clever and confident in his actions. I watched him with the admiration of a younger brother totally enraptured by his charisma. Everyone simply did what he wished. When he would show up in the middle of the night at my aunt's house, even though she disapproved, she would smile and shake her head as though he were a young child doing silly pranks. Then she would take care of him, prepare food for him, or provide him with a quick shower. He spoke so naturally and directly even though we all knew he was hiding his short AK-47 under his jacket, along with his pistol. On nights when he didn't need me, he would stay for a few hours and talk and then disappear.

Mohammed, my brother, and me (Dr. Bewar)

His demeanor began to change, though. He was no longer as carefree and confident. He seemed to always be watching his back and jumping at shadows. He explained that many of his comrades were disappearing. Some were arrested, while others were just gone. Those who were arrested were taken away and never heard from again either. Mohammed remained too aloof even from his own commanders to be caught, though. He had his own plans, so it would seem, and so he decided that he would disappear also but on his own terms. Without a note or a word of goodbye, he simply vanished from our lives. We knew that he had planned this. Nonetheless, it still worried us to not know where he was or if something had ruined his plans. He was able to hide and survive for a year without being caught. All the rest of his companions eventually were sold out, killed, or imprisoned and then killed. But he was able to finally escape to the mountains, and he finally got word to us that he was safe, but that we would not see him for a while and to please take care of his wife and children.

These late-night excursions into clandestine rebellious activities made me so patriotic to Kurdistan. I knew very little about the politics of the matter, but I had read about the history and had heard so many stories, and had seen for myself the injustice and cruelty of the government. I was proud to be doing some small service. After hiding out for a year, though, Mohammed was suddenly arrested by his own Kurdish Communist Party for some unknown reason and was sentenced to prison. He disappeared from my life again. Though I didn't see him again for many years, his reckless bravery and determination inspired me in ways that I would have never imagined. I finally did see him again, but it wasn't until I joined the PUK Party as a Peshmerga myself.

So I was becoming a man. My father had shown me what a true man was, and my brothers had formed my ethics. From Bakir, I learned to work and be responsible. From Burhan, I learned to think and reason. And from Mohammed, I gained my sense of rebellion and fighting spirit.

Learning about all the hostilities from empires and regimes throughout history perpetrated against all the Kurdish people in

Kurdistan broke my heart. It also confused and enraged me; why should we have been treated like that? What had we done? Why were we still being treated this way? From all that I read, I realized that we had been living on our own land for thousands of years, but in all that history, we had always been told how we had to live our lives. Despite such a long and ancient history, we had been left stateless; we had boundaries and borders that were routinely ignored. We had cultures and traditions that were mocked and scorned. We had our own language that was suppressed and often forbidden. Our fertile land had been divided into pieces which were squabbled over and occupied by outside kingdoms, empires, and republics. Our land had never really been ours; it was always controlled by outside forces.

I wasn't alone in this feeling, though. Even my parents and other family members considered the injustice of our plight. All the villages lived this feeling, and though they rarely spoke of it openly (traitors were everywhere), it was a very poorly kept secret that everyone wanted independence. In fact, there were secret radio programs that would broadcast every evening about the resistance, recent atrocities, and even Kurdish music and poetry that were very anti-Iraqi. Every day and night, whenever I had time, I would read, listen, or watch (in later years when we finally got television) anything pertaining to my people. Listening to the forbidden Kurdish opposition parties in hiding was making my young teenage blood boil. I had visions of joining the resistance, the Peshmerga, to fight for the rights of my identity as a Kurd. Every afternoon between 4:00 p.m. and 6:00 p.m., we listened to a Kurdish radio broadcast about recent Peshmerga activities. Sometimes, when my family was especially nervous, but I still had to know, I would listen to it on very low volume so no one would know. I would put the radio up to my ear so I could understand what the broadcaster was saying. It gave me such great pleasure to listen to how brave our Peshmerga were in fighting the Iraqi military regime.

The radio program was run by a secret group of rebels. The government was constantly trying to shut them down, but they were quick and resourceful. While we were listening, we would start to hear the station become fuzzy with static. It was the government causing static interference to the station. When it became too difficult to listen, we would start searching for the different frequencies. The broadcasters, when they found they were being jammed, would quickly switch to another frequency. The government would eventually find this station as well, so they would play this constant game of cat and mouse. They would change the static and then the channel again. As a listener, you would just have to listen and then change the channel periodically to find the new station. Hopefully, you could find it faster than the government so you could listen for a while before the government would start to scramble the channel.

Besides news of the resistance, there were brave cultural icons who used their talents to further our cause. I remember how excited I used to get when the famous Kurdish singer Shivan Perwer, would come out with a new album. Each song would be about the Kurdish struggle, both historical and current. You could only listen to it in hiding, and you had to make sure people you do not trust did not know you were listening. I had a cassette player. When the cassette named *Keena em*, which means "Who are we?" in Kurdish, came out, I acquired it quickly, and it was something I would listen to repeatedly and never got tired of.

We knew very well that if the government found out what we were listening to and what we were reading, they would persecute us with confiscations, imprisonments, and possibly even hanging! As a young man, though my blood boiled over the information I was consuming about how the government treated our people and youth throughout Kurdistan, I was more overcome with anger than any fear of getting caught. It felt like a fire that only grew with the fuel I poured on it. My rebellious antigoverment nationalistic actions were justified within my conscience. I now felt I could see clearly how the government was systematically taking our identity away and crushing our rights. One example stands out firmly in my mind: I remember reading about the *Arabization* policy, forced migration of the Kurdish people and redistribution of our Kurdish land to incoming Arabic families. This happened particularly in regions where Kurdish people were a majority and had some powers and authority which the national government wanted to undermine. In the regions such as Kirkuk, Mosul, and Khanaqeen, thousands of families were displaced. As a young Kurd, I came to understand the local saying "There are no friends except the mountains." This was a saying we had to show that politically, socially, nationally, and even security-wise, the Kurds have only ever been used by the superpowers that come in contact with them. There are no long-term allies that have supported us and stayed constant. So we say we only have our mountains as friends. No one will support us or help us to enjoy the rights and freedoms that others around the world have enjoyed. The mountains were always our refuge, stronghold, and final defense. We have always had to fight for our most basic cultural, national, and personal rights. That is why I was fascinated by my Kurdish history. It was hurtful to read about my ancient ancestors without their own rights or freedoms and realizing that nothing had changed. We still didn't have a state or country of our own. Knowing Kurdistan was known as the cradle of civilization was both a proud moment for me and a statement of insult knowing that we were still oppressed. Everything about our land held mystery and history behind it, and all those ancient voices seemed to swell up inside of me and demand freedom.

Struggle of Ideologies

As I mentioned before, I was learning about history, but I was ignorant of politics. I didn't understand the warring factions even between my own Kurdish nation. One event affected this knowledge and influenced many decisions for me later in life. It was 1983, and I was still a boy of about fourteen. The Kurdish political and armed opposition parties were busy fighting with each other. This was commonly referred to by the Kurdish people as "Bra Kuzhi"—"Brother killing brother" or "Fighting each other in the mountains." They were killing each other over political power even without being recognized by the Iraqi government as having any actual legal legitimacy in the country.

The Peshmerga who had volunteered to fight for this cause had done so because they thought they were supposed to fight their enemy, the Iraqi dictator. Instead, they were only killing their brothers. The Iraqi government was happy to let them battle it out without interference. The Iraqi referred to them officially as *mukharbeen*, a loose translation for the English word *subversive, rebellious*, or *insurrectionary*). The factions were so ideological that they would not back down, and each side blamed the other for starting the fight.

Nevertheless, for the Kurdish people, it did not matter; what mattered the most was that their sons agreed to carry arms to fight the Iraqi government to free the Kurdish people and establish equality within Iraq. Because of this, a lot of misinformation and rival feelings developed which led to their sons getting killed by their Kurdish brothers. This civil war started early in the 1980s and continued until 1987 when the parties finally ended the conflict and decided to engage the Iraqi regime instead. They signed an agreement to stop the fighting. This was due to the Iraqi regime's campaign, led by Saddam Hussein, that was determined to push them out of the borders of Iraq. This was known as the Anfal campaign.

The PUK, the Kurdish faction that ruled in my area of Kurdistan, started negotiations in 1983 with the Iraqi government. According to many politburos, it was because their strategy was stretching thin and their fighters were desperately in need of a rest from fighting since the PUK had been embroiled in fighting with their neighboring Kurdish faction, the PDK, a Kurdish Social Party, and the Iraqi Communist Party. In 1983, the PUK with bolstered support from the Iraqi regime started detaining non-PUK members within their reach. Some of my family members were accused and arrested when I was still in those formative years. My two older brothers, Bakir and Burhan, along with my father, were taken to prison. The PUK argued that the reason behind this was because Mohammed, my eldest brother, was a Peshmerga with the Communist Party and allegedly had been harassing PUK family members somewhere else. Of course, the allegation was baseless, but at that time, the PUK was trying to show their muscles to the local villagers and any families that had Peshmerga on the other side; they were, in essence, harassing us. The irony was, though he hid it from Iraqi officials, my older brother Bakir was quite obvious to everyone else openly supporting the local PUK effort and loved their leader, Jalal Talabani. And to show his love for Mr. Talabani, who was the secretary of general of the PUK, he named their new baby girl after Mr. Talabani's wife, whose name is Hero.

None of this mattered to the PUK officials; they detained my family members for more than two weeks. After taking my brothers and my father, I was the only male old enough to become responsible for our family affairs. As it happened a day after some PUK members traveled around our areas freely since they were in negotiation with the Iraqi government, one of their high-ranking members visited our village. He was eating lunch with one of their member's family; his name was Saeed. I went there with my mother to speak with the guy; his name was Mamosta Ahmed. Even at that young age, I was full of righteous indignation. Here was a man who was betraying the trust of his people. We were supposed to be fighting for our independence, and he had taken my father!

(from right Dr. Bewar, and his brothers- Burhan, Abdulkhaliq and Jamal)

To his face, I started very harshly criticizing the PUK action of taking my family members. I boldly stood in front of this man and demanded, "What gives you the right to take all of my adult male family members? Who would do such a thing? You and your party are supposed to assist the Kurdish people, not create a crisis. You are taking my family members based on an allegation against my older brother while they have no control over him whatsoever." Sometime later on, my family members were released; Bakir was the last to be freed.

Years later—after leaving Kurdistan and my migration to the United States, on a return visit to Kurdistan to visit my family—my older brother Mohammed came to visit me at my mother's home. He brought Mamosta Ahmed with him to eat lunch with us. He asked him, "Do you recognize this young man?"

Mamosta said, "No, but I know he is your brother and came back from America to visit you."

Mohammed said, "Do you remember in 1983 when you detained my family members because of me when I was with the Communist Party? You were eating lunch at Saeed's house? My mother and my youngest brother came to talk to you? That was Kamal! This is him, Kamal."

Mamosta Ahmed said he remembered me very well. He remarked that I was a brilliant and sharp young man. He confessed that I had made him feel guilty about the party (PUK) taking our family members. He had been struck by the audacity of this boy openly criticizing the PUK. He turned to my brother and explained that I had touched on a few points about Mohammed and the unfairness of detaining three individuals from one family under a pretext which they had no control over. At this point in our conversation, he turned back to me with great respect, "Well," he said, "welcome back to Kurdistan, Kamal. Now, as you see, Mohammed is a PUK Peshmerga, one of us, and we are very good friends. And I want to apologize for the past event."

Chapter 3

Daya w Baba

I recently took my son back to Kurdistan to see my family and to my mother. He got to see the land I grew up in and experience the beautiful culture that cradled me. I spent long hours talking with my mother and expressed my love and honor to her. It was such a blessing to be able to be with her. Though I was happy to see my whole family, I still felt the empty space in my heart where my father was missing. Oh, how I wish I could introduce him to his grandson. That he could take him in his strong embrace and show him the same love that I was surrounded by my whole childhood. It is the nature of children to not notice what they have when they are young. They never fully appreciate the sacrifices of time, money, and opportunity that are willingly offered on their behalf so they might have life. I will never be able to adequately thank my mother. However, being a parent myself, I have some notion of what she gave for me, but for my father, I only understood the man and father he was after it was too late to tell him. I pray that he somehow knows how I feel, though.

Though this section may seem out of place here, it is imperative that you understand the incredible caliber of people that I was born to and raised by. Two of the greatest people I have ever known were my mother and father (*Daya w Baba*). They were strong and gentle, passionate and calm, stalwart and meek. The choices I made and whom I have become are so wrapped up in the examples and support

I received from these two people that, without knowing about them, you would have a difficult time understanding who I am.

My mother

Mother… I speak several languages and have a doctorate degree. Yet with all that education and with all those languages, I still cannot find words which adequately describe or give a sufficient description to such a great name. *Compassion*, *love*, and *care* are all related words associated with *mother*. It is something so precious in the hearts of so many people that, without it, life would have been impossible. Throughout history, mothers have always been cited as the key to the personal achievement of the noblest and greatest figures.

After many years of living in the United States, I came to realize that I had simply taken the love of my mother toward me for granted. I assumed her strong emotional instinct as merely a duty she was to offer. In my mind, whenever I had a little pain in part of my world and when I was complaining about it, I was expecting the response would automatically trigger my mother's compassion in a way that would make me feel better knowing that for the time being, someone cared. I had such a selfish mind. In many cases, no matter how far away my mother was located, I would find refuge in her support and love. Even when I was halfway around the world in the US and she was all the way back in Kurdistan of Iraq, distance could not affect my decision to seek her voice. In every event of my life, especially during tough times, but even with small personal issues as a young lonely immigrant to the US, I would take refuge in my mother's voice and seek that personal connection only a mother can give to recuperate my brief distress.

My mother—Khadija

Years later, after getting married and having a son, Ari, I realized how selfish I had been throughout my life. I had never thought about the many personal difficulties my mother had suffered in her life. Despite losing three young children to disease and war, working her body to exhaustion, and supporting a large unruly family that seemed to constantly be putting themselves into mortal danger, she never complained. And I, instead of supporting her emotionally, just sought her affection and emotional support. I guess losing three young children was not enough! There was me, the one who is still alive but who was a constant burden on her shoulders and mind. Despite being far away at war, as a refugee and then as an immigrant. I did not see that for years until, I believe, after Ari was born. My worldview suddenly shifted dramatically. When I reflect on my love toward Ari, I realize why my mother never complained about my needs all these years whenever I was complaining. I now understood that, as parents, regardless of the age of your child or children, the love we have toward them is unconditional.

What bothers me the most, when I reflect on my past, was how unappreciative I was. Often, whenever she would display emotion toward me, I felt I did not need it, and it would somehow annoy me! For a young boy and especially an independent teenager, too much emotion and affection toward me was embarrassing. Fortunately, from her point of view, it did not matter to frustrate the mind of a young and inexperienced son occasionally. Ironically, today, I see how Ari gets annoyed when I perform such acts, in particular, in a public place when people are around. It takes me a minute or two to realize I need to stop my public show of affection, but at other times, I ignore that because I just can't help but love him.

Now my mother is getting rather old. As I think about the past and how strong she was while she was working on the farm, I remember watching her out in the hot summer sun, pregnant during Ramadan. She was so full of faith that, even though she was not required to fast, she still fasted all through the day. As a boy and young man, it was difficult for me to be able to complain about needing to fast when my mother kept a determined smile on her face and worked twice as hard as me. Then without complaint, she would go directly to the house to prepare our night meals, feed us, and take care of the household chores at the same time. She would arise earlier than anyone else in the morning so that food would be prepared, and then she would be off to the fields again.

Today, her once-strong body is old, and her spirit longs to be with my father. It hurts me to see what time does to the human beings I love. Seeing my mother being fed by my little sister as I so often saw her feeding one of my younger siblings. That pain by itself is excruciating when I see that life's cycle is reversing.

Throughout my life, I have always said that it would be very rare to find such a mentally and physically strong woman like my mother. Years of experience have shown me that it is not easy to completely crush the soul of someone who is full of hope and aspiration.

My father

Within my family, I always felt closer to my father than anybody else did. My father was my teacher, my guide, and, above all, my friend and my mentor. I knew my father loved each of us. However, the way he interacted with me, I could feel how much he loved me personally and individually, just as he loved all his children. I know if he were still alive, he would be proud of what I have accomplished in life and how hard I have worked throughout my life to be where I am in the United States. Nevertheless, I suspect he would have some disappointment as well in the way that I have turned to not being a religious person. To him, being a good person was something that came from religion. I understand that this notion is common among many cultures. However, I believe religion is something too personal. To be a good member of society and a good person, you do not have to be religious. Based on my experiences, I've known many individuals who thought they were devoted to their beliefs and religion but were actually doing the opposite. Cheating, stealing, and committing different kinds of "sins"; they are okay with that as long as their society or community does not find out about it. My father's faith and honor, however, were pure. He truly tried to live as he believed. He did not cheat or lie or steal. He was patient and calm with his children. In a culture that permitted fathers to beat their children, he was merciful and never raised his hand against us. The only time he touched us was with love to kiss us. He would call me to him, and I would lie on his lap while he stroked my head. Those are the powerful memories that remind me that there are people who truly live their religion. We always had a special relationship. Years later after my father had passed away, my mother told me that after his stroke he had not been fully aware of what was going on. He would often call out for me from his hospital bed. When my mother would explain that I was not able to come, he would smile reassuringly and explain that if Allah wants my boy to hear me, he will hear me. For years, I would have dreams of my father coming to talk with me, and we would sit for hours and talk just as I did as a small boy. These dreams were not disturbing but were, in fact, reassuring that I had not lost him completely and he was still in my heart. For years after I lost my father, I dreamt of him. In my dream, we would talk about different things in life. Often, I wake up in the middle of the night. I find myself alone and wonder if what I was experiencing was really only a dream.

My father's traits and personality were rare in his community and even in his family. He was not a graduate of Yale or any kind of school of philosophy. However, to most of the people in our community, his leadership was incomparable. I myself have learned so many lessons in life from him: respect, manners, wisdom, peace, and many other positive attributes. He wanted to enrich others' lives to reach their potential. Such a leadership trait showed me to never be selfish when it comes to doing the right thing. He was truly a servant leader! He was very humble; and no matter how old individuals were, whether it was the imam of our mosque or his youngest child, during his conversation, he would actively listen, and he made sure they got his full attention.

My father—Haji Ismail

The biggest gift he had was his ability to solve problems. People in our community would come to him when they had an issue, usually a complex issue that they were unable to resolve without assistance. In our village, we didn't really have a magistrate or judge. People would seek out a wise neighbor who could help them in disputes. My father was often chosen to be that mediator. Without hesitation, he would make time for anyone to ensure his or her problem was solved. I admired his passion and his way of handling such delicate issues. More often than not, he would come out with both sides listening to him when he talked and gave them an option in order to reconcile their current issue. The way he influenced others, I could not see anyone else that was able to carry such a task so skillfully. Persuading others was a natural trait of his in the process of solving community issues. My father had to carry such a task often in our village and throughout our region. I secretly thought that if he could be paid for all the community problem-solving he did, we would not have to work on the farm anymore. Nevertheless, he believed in the duty he was asked to do for the good of our people and the community.

Throughout my life, especially when I was reflecting, I considered myself very lucky to have been born to parents who loved me so much. In particular, to have a father so perfect that devoted his life to caring and loving us so much. Thinking back to the way he was carrying a simple conversation, there were always lessons to be learned, and that was one thing no one can understand. Even for me, it was beyond my comprehension.

There was never a second of hesitation to go to him when I had a question, because there was no doubt in my mind that he could supply me with higher wisdom that I seldom could see or get from anybody else. Years later when he died and I knew I had lost him forever, I knew that my greatest teacher had died. I always wondered if I could have a second chance at this life (even though that is impossible), without hesitation, I would reenroll in the special school under the tutelage of the greatest educator I ever knew with the hope of graduating in the school I never had the chance to complete.

I know I was blessed in that sense to have had a father so genuine and so pure. He lived a simple life, but he was always grateful for what he had. Such examples have disappeared in my life since I left my home country. I know, however, that what he taught me will never be forgotten. Nevertheless, a longer time around him would have given me a further understanding and the meaning of life.

Dad, I know you left us over twenty years ago, but the time has not changed anything in my heart for the love of your fatherhood, caring, and, above all, teaching me to be noble and brave in life—because everything has an end in life except our good deeds and our individual's sheer character while we breathe in this temporary journey through life.

Historical Note on the Peshmerga

When I reflect on my adventurous spirit during my teenage years, I shudder inwardly at the memories. I am pretty sure I could not do anything like that today—the risks I took, with disregard for my own safety or life or to the consequences to my mother or father should something dire happen to me. As a father, having my son, Ari, I would do anything to stop him from doing what I did in the past to ensure his safety. At that time, however, I was invincible. Thoughts of heroism, patriotism, revenge, and destiny filled my mind. My future was full of glory, and everything was in my mind except dying. I was anxious to show the people of my village and everyone else that I was a man and ready for the next chapter of my life.

Every nation uses the impetuous fervor of youth to drive its ambitions. Revolutions flourish on college campuses for this very reason. Young people so recently freed from the shackles of childhood stretch their wings against the caged bars that stifle their progress. Life is spread before them like an open field running in all directions while death is not even a distant mountain on the horizon. They will not die—they cannot die. So it was with the Kurdish people. Young Kurdish boys were propelled by their nature to join a movement to resist the very real oppression of their families, their fortunes, and their futures. In Kurdistan, these fighters were called the Peshmerga. *Peshmerga* was a revered term used for nearly a century to identify those protectors of the Kurdish people and our land. The name started in the 1940s, when the Kurdish rebellion started against the Iraqi monarchy. In Kurdish, the term means "those who face death." It is only used in the Kurdistan of Iraq and Iran for Kurdish young revolutionaries who opposed the Iraqi and Iranian regimes. It was really only used by the Kurds since the government during Saddam's regime labeled the Peshmerga as a *mukharib*, which means *destructor*, *saboteur*, or *destroyer*. The Kurdish people, however, were freedom fighters and liberators.

It was only years later that the name became known internationally. After ISIS took over a swath of land in Iraq and Syria in 2014, the name especially became popular throughout the world. The Peshmerga were an instrumental force able to stand up and fight against the ISIS brutality with the support of the US and its allies in the war on terror. Just when it seemed that they were no longer needed because of the regime changes in Iraq, the war against ISIS started the Peshmerga again, and once again, it hit me personally. My brother was part of the force that fought those evil forces (ISIS); and my cousin and best friend, Aziz, was martyred by ISIS when he was fighting them in the Mosul region.

All of that happened years later, though, and my only knowledge at the time was of the two boys hunted in our village from my childhood. My older brother Mohammed's secret missions in Erbil and the forbidden radio broadcasts we tried to listen to. All of which was enough to stir those revolutionary feelings in my emerging male mind.

What did it mean to be a Peshmerga? Before I became a Peshmerga, the name itself meant a lot to me. It was an organization: holy and divine. I considered them more saintly than our *mulas* or religious leaders. There were many personal reasons this group of rebels held such a fanatic reverence in my soul. First was my older brother. As I mentioned before, he was a Peshmerga. The love and adoration of a younger sibling I had for my older brother is how my passion started with the Peshmerga. In addition, I was Kurdish. I was proud of my heritage and my culture. My father and mother had raised me to understand who we were in the world. So I, like the general Kurdish population, had unconditional love for the young rebel warriors. When a person is willing to sacrifice his or her life for the cause, that tells you a lot about that person's dedication. It is evident that their determination runs more profoundly than a simple fantasy or whim.

I will start with the two brothers who caused the uproar on my first day of school. I, like the other boys my age, was fascinated with these rebels. They were the Peshmerga whom we talked about in hushed tones, that, as boys, we pretended to be as we mock-attacked our oppressors, the ones who were martyred in the villages surrounding us. These men were so determined in their struggles for the Kurdish nation that I placed them in a position of reverence in my young mind—indeed, in the minds of our entire nation. That willingness to die for others was precisely what the Peshmerga were doing for their people and their country. The survival of our nation depended on the name and the existence of this "Holy Spirit" that protected Kurdistan from tyranny. How could anything go wrong when I became one of them and my wish finally turned into reality? I often mused that nothing would make me happier than joining those Kurdish national heroes. The feeling was so real toward becoming a Peshmerga that I could often taste the scent of battle and victory in my dreams. It seemed even the Iraqi regime and its soldiers were scared of these brave revolutionaries. They fought like lions during the fighting.

Such were the visions and illusions of this mighty force, the protectors of my home. They were bathed in glorified light, and it seemed that such heroism could not fail to succeed. Sacrifices were done without pain, it seemed. All were loyal and brave. There was no retreat, no faltering; there would be no surrender once I joined. Surely, how could any of these titans surrender to such cowards as the Iraqi regime? Such were my musings and fantasies. It took only a few experiences, however, after joining the force, until I could see why so many of the people who joined the army quickly went back to the Iraqi government and surrendered.

In reality, becoming one of the Peshmerga and joining the revolution was hard to do. It meant hunger, often going without food for days. It meant very little sleep on uncomfortable mats, sheds, and the bare earth. It meant walking and walking to and from campaigns to send messages and to set up new posts. Trudging along dirt roads and forest paths for days and months from mountain to mountain in old boots alone by yourself meant being always dirty. The dust clung to your sweaty body, and there were no showers for months. You were, indeed, fortunate if you got a chance to wash yourself and your clothes.

Being a rebel fighter was the hardest during the wintertime. During the winter, you were always cold. There was never enough winter gear to go around. You took turns sharing sleeping bags and keeping watch. Cleaning was even less likely in the winter, so a Peshmerga was lucky if he showered once or twice the whole season. The worst was the lice. Your hair and clothes were always full of this pernicious pest. Sharing bedding and not cleaning meant the parasites were on every soldier. You were continually itching your hair and body. It was so hard to resist. Often, we had to be mindful of such an inadvertent move especially when we as Peshmerga were scattered all over a village in their homes to eat lunch or dinner. Spreading lice was a poor reward to the kind villagers who sacrificed their food for us.

Your best friend was the night in the mountains. The darkness surrounded you like a shield to protect you so you could carry out your guerilla fights against one of the most powerful regimes in the Middle East. You must hide during the day and only come out at night. Watch yourself every second, night and day—making sure you did not expose yourself during the day to the public. If you did, it would mean you had to fight. Discovery meant military helicopters, machine guns, and fighting until your last bullet was spent and then running like hell.

As a teenager, I knew nothing of this, only the glory. This glory road, therefore, seemed the only path my feet could follow. Therefore, toward the end of 1986, before I was eighteen, my friend and I had finally made up our minds to join the Peshmerga. After years of reading about the injustices and seeing the cruelty and experiencing firsthand the brutality of the Iraqi regime, we secretly formed a pact that we would join the resistance. It was near the end of a cold and wet November when we planned to set out. After hearing about the many sacrifices our fellow brothers were going through for our independence, we wanted to volunteer to fight for the Kurdish cause, and we were willing to sacrifice our lives if necessary. At the time, I felt I was a grown man and ready for whatever would happen, and so at such a young and naïve age, we put what we called a plan into action. I say it was a plan, but in reality, there was very little planning involved.

My friend and I did not care about the consequences of this journey or what our decision would mean to us or our families once we moved in that direction. We didn't even tell our families for fear of being stopped. I remember it was about noon when we started walking from our village in the direction my friend believed we could find the Peshmerga forces to join. (Since it was a resistance force, their bases and operations were kept secret, but for the Kurds, it was a fairly open secret.) Our families were kept completely in the dark. I already had one brother who had joined the freedom fighters, and he had almost been killed numerous times because of it, and it had cost my father a fair bit of wealth to free him. I knew that if my mother or father found out what we were planning, they would never let us go. It was not because they opposed the Peshmerga or they were not patriotic enough to our Kurdish nationality. Rather, it was due to our safety. They knew very well that it would probably mean a cold death for us, and for them, it could mean persecution and torture to have a son fighting for the resistance. My father and mother, along with my other older brothers, knew the concept of joining the Kurdish forces was not a safe idea.

In November, the rains come to Kurdistan, and it turns bitterly cold as fall braces for winter. I remember we had decided to leave during the afternoon so that it would look like we were just going for a walk. If we left too early, it would arouse suspicion; and if we left late, we knew we might be caught in the cold wet night alone on the Kurdish highway stranded between any villages. We could not really take anything with us, for that would arouse suspicion as well. In our village, the weather was still fairly nice, so we didn't think it would look right if we went on a "walk" wearing gear for cold weather.

Also, it was after lunch, so we couldn't pack food for our journey because our moms would know we were up to something. As I said, we thought we had a plan when in reality we were just walking away from home completely unprepared.

As we walked, we had to keep an ear and eye open to the horizon, always wary of the sounds of chopper engines. One of the scariest things that could happen to us was for an Iraqi military helicopter to spot travelers, especially boys, on a lonely road. They would, indeed, shoot us to death. Every day, three helicopters flew over various Kurdish regions. Whenever they saw someone walking away from a village, car, or motorcycle, they would swoop low and start firing their machine guns. Men, women, children, it didn't matter to the helicopters anyone could get killed. It did not matter even if they were poor civilian farmers with tractor problems. If you were walking along a deserted road, it meant you were a rebel and the military could gun you down. I really believe many of the soldiers just wanted to kill Kurds. So many innocent people died horribly from the Iraqi military, so as we walked now, we had to watch carefully to avoid that happening to us.

We walked for four to five hours while the weather stayed nice. We were feeling confident and free now. Our plan was set in motion, and we had no plans to back out. As we walked, we talked about what it would be like to fight for our people. We dreamed aloud about the heroic deeds we would perform and the victorious welcome we would receive as our forces triumphed over the evil dictator. Our banter buoyed our spirits, and for those first few hours, the marching was light and exciting. We soon arrived in a neighboring village where some family of another friend of ours lived. This village was much closer to the main Erbil and Kirkuk highways, so it was a natural stop for us. Many of the families knew each other, and we were excited to see some people we knew. They, in turn, were also surprised and happy to see us and invited us to dinner, as was customary. After we had eaten, the father and mother asked us what we were doing in the area so far from home and at such a late hour. We proudly boasted that we were going to join the Peshmerga.

We were expecting some minor resistance, and then we thought they would ultimately be proud that we had chosen such a noble path. It was surprising to us then to see how worried and anxious they became. I remember the mother pleaded with us to go home to our parents. They tried every way they could think to convince us of the price that we would pay for joining. They recounted the dangers we would face and how sad our families would be when we died. If we had not been so young or had not been together, these pleas may have wavered our resolve, but we had promised each other and were stubbornly determined to fight. We politely refused their idea and thanked them for the food, then we left, knowing that if we stayed the night, our resolve might not be so strong in the morning.

We started walking away from the village. The lights and warmth faded quickly into the gathering dark. It was now getting quite cold. We didn't have coats or gloves or anything but our regular clothes. We walked quietly for about an hour until, on the road ahead of us, we saw a group of men approaching. They were armed but obviously not Iraqi soldiers. We knew at once that they were a group of Peshmerga that was going in the opposite direction from us. They stopped in front of us, a little surprised to see two young men walking the road by night. They knew we were Kurds, and so they wondered where we were going. My friend and I told them in prideful and excited tones, "We are coming to join *you*." They laughed, saying, "Welcome." They half expected us to fall in line and march with them. However, my friend and I had a destination in mind. One of our other friends who had joined the Peshmerga earlier told us where we should go to join. We relayed this information to the men, and they wished us the best and then continued their march past us. This meeting was so different from the village experience. These men were our heroes. They risked everything to bring freedom and dignity to our land. They were so young and yet full of life and vigor. They laughed and joked as they walked. This was the vision we had imagined. Such men, such warriors, soon we would be joining them. We walked taller for a bit after this meeting, unconsciously imitating the confident swagger and careless banter of the fighters. Our destination was still at least another day away walking; however, our faces were more directed and our steps more sure. We knew where we were going.

We were so determined—nothing was going to stop us from going to join the Peshmerga. What we were seeing and hearing daily of the struggles and injustices drove us to fight for our land and people. What the government was doing to the Kurdish people was an atrocity that could not be forgotten. In the mind of any Kurdish person who had a little bit of Kurdishness in them, it was impossible to not side with the Kurdish cause. The daily news was spread among the villages of how the government was oppressing the people, manipulating the education of the youth, and even indiscriminately killing young and old. The Iraqi government was systematically bombarding villages and then attacking the region to detain civilians. Some would never be seen again while others were moved to concentration camps. There were so many instances of such horrid proportions it would be impossible to tell them all, but one of the most well-known was the genocide of the Barzani Tribe. On a whim, it seemed, the Iraqi military took more than eight thousand people from their homes, fields, and businesses. They were all male and, therefore, traditionally the breadwinners for their families. None of the eight thousand were ever seen again. Most likely, their bodies were dropped into one of the many mass graves that still dot the region. I remember the tragic stories of how these families struggled in the town of Qushtepe. They were all female, but now with no men in their family or village, they had to work and do whatever they had to do to survive. In Kurdish culture, the family unit was so important, and each member had distinct duties and obligations. The loss of so many workers was devastating. All of Kurdistan recognized this act by the Iraqi regime as a plan specifically to dishonor the Kurdish family structure and undermine its culture. Besides the kidnapping and killing, there was an overarching well-known systemic Arabization of the Kurds. Even today, many people assume that all people in the Middle East are Arabic. This is untrue. Each region has its own ethnicity and heritage. The Kurds had a language, culture, and customs that the governing countries systematically sought to destroy. This Arabization tactic simply changed the demographics of villages and towns by forcing the removal of Kurdish families in Kirkuk, Khanaqeen, and Sinjar areas. The families were scattered throughout different regions of the country to weaken their collective sense of culture. This government policy did not start with Saddam. In fact, such a policy had been in place for years and years even before Saddam took over power, but under his leadership, it seemed to increase tremendously.

These atrocities were well understood within the Kurdish community and especially in the rural areas and small villages. If it had not been for these despicable actions by the government the rebel movement would have quickly failed. The whole support for the Peshmerga forces fell on the villagers' shoulders. As rebel forces, they had no financial backing, manufacturing for guns, ammunition, uniforms, or vehicles. They couldn't farm or buy food. The Peshmerga were completely dependent on the support of the locals. This aid was freely and honorably given because of the stories of such abuses that circulated among them. As the war continued and the government continued to try to crack down on the forces, they soon saw that it would be impossible to defeat these forces in their retreats because they were warned, harbored, fed, and clothed by the small communities where they were welcomed so freely. The government, therefore, decided to focus on these villages that were providing them with shelter and food. They started destroying the logistical support for the Peshmerga forces by attacking the villages. By the end of the conflict, they had razed more than four thousand villages to the ground, including my home village of Peerdawood.

All of these thoughts went through my mind as we walked. It was quite late now, and we were starting to rethink our decision to walk away from home without even jackets. In addition, the light rains in the village were turning to winter blasts the higher up in the mountains we got. Our hands and feet were wet and numb. I couldn't feel my ears anymore. Late into the night, we stumbled into another village. We stopped and randomly went to one of the houses in the village. They saw two frozen boys shivering on their doorstep and immediately invited us in. They fed us graciously while we told them who we were and why we were there. They offered us mats to sleep on. Before we fell asleep, though, another group of Peshmerga showed up; and they, too, were fed and sheltered. These poor villagers—already struggling to subsist on meager supplies for themselves and their families, living in poor shelters with dirt floors—were so quick to help those who fought for freedom on the mere hope that someday they might have their own nation and be able to work, speak, and live in the manner they cherished.

The next morning, the family fed us again; and we left them with our thanks and headed to the Peshmerga headquarters of the Erbil region, which was responsible for all the resistance efforts for our region. Kosrat Ali was the main person in charge of the region, a member of the politburo of the PUK. For the Kurdish resistance, there were two major Kurdish parties, the Patriotic Union of Kurdistan (PUK) and the Kurdistan Democratic Party (PDK). I joined the PUK. It had been more recently established (1976) and better aligned with my personal belief that the party should not be controlled by a particular person, family, or tribe. On the other hand, the PDK party, historically, had been Barazani's family; and even to this day, no one else can be a president of the party, and they will never allow anyone to lead the party no matter how capable that person is in terms of politics. Nevertheless, in the recent history of PUK, I have witnessed the same attitude by the Talabani's family toward the PUK party that it is becoming more of a family party as well.

Now that we were high up in the mountains, winter had already arrived. The mountains were blanketed with white snow everywhere. We hiked all morning and into the late afternoon before finally arriving at the secret headquarters. It had turned very cold as the sun started to set, so when we finally arrived at headquarters, we were offered food and drinks. In addition, they offered us warm jackets; they had been donated by the villages. I remember mine was green. It was my first Peshmerga "uniform," and I loved it! Of course, we did not have official uniforms here, but it felt like I was finally enlisting. Besides that, I also felt a lot warmer, which I appreciated as well.

Now that the excitement of running away to join the resistance was ebbing, reality started to set in. My first week and throughout the month were very hard. Every day, I was second-guessing my decision to join. I was going through separation anxiety being away from family. I had always lived in a house full of loving brothers and sisters and a caring mother and wise father. Suddenly, all that was gone. What I missed the most was coming home and the food was ready to eat. Being a Peshmerga, we had to go to people's houses in the villages and have them feed us. We had few provisions in camp, and since the food all came from the nearest villages, it was just easier to go there to eat. Most often, we separated so we were alone or in small groups; that way we wouldn't overwhelm any one family. I believe in most cases, the people were very welcoming and kind. They gave us food, shelter, and nice, warm beds. It's very hard to imagine how some of the families must have felt when unannounced guests show up in the middle of the night, and you were expected to take care of them and be welcoming no matter what time it was or whether you even had enough food. As a Kurd, you were expected to share everything with them.

After one month of staying there, I started feeling comfortable with the group. Knowing each other better and understanding the leadership made me feel that way. There was no training here, though. I was never trained to learn how to shoot or how to fight the ruthless Iraqi government. We didn't do marching drills or drills of any kind. We just had to learn as we could from those willing to share, and then they just told us to do our best during the actual fighting. We were under the command of Ali Masifi, who was the head of the unit in charge of the place. Ali was not a very imposing figure. He was neither tall nor short, though he had a huge beard. He always wore the Kurdish traditional clothes "Rank u Choghal." I saw him as a very humble leader, and this simple leadership engendered so much respect from his comrades. I remember him most because he always made a lot of us laugh during the harsh winter, usually while we were playing dominos together.

Then they transferred me to another place, a smaller unit which Fuad Rash was in charge of. I did not have anything to say or could say anything about the transfer. The rule was when someone joins the Peshmerga, the leader of the region, such as Ali Masifi, makes the decision on where that person can go. In that case, the unit I was sent to needed more Peshmerga, and that's why I was sent there. The winter was harsh, and it was snowing all the time. Where I was born, in my village, we did not have that much snow. It was much warmer than the place of my unit. The cold weather was killing me. I didn't have good shoes, and it seemed that we were always outside and, most of the time, snow. After arriving there, Fuad Rash managed to procure me a pair of better walking shoes. I did not care what kind of shoes they were; I just needed better shoes. Since he had gotten me a new pair of shoes, he asked me to join him on his tours around his district. We didn't have transportation, vehicles, or animals. So we simply walked everywhere we needed to go. Rash was in charge of the Khoshnawati District. He was responsible for visiting all parts of the region to ensure its security. That was the first day of my travel all over part of the Khoshnawati District, walking every day during the coldest part of the winter. We were about five Peshmerga, including our leader, Fuad Rash. Our survey took us more than a month of daily walking. Each morning, we would rise, eat, and then start walking. We would stay at night in whichever of the villages we came to last. We would invite ourselves into one of the houses in the village. They would always feed us and provide sleeping mats and shelter.

That month was the longest of my life. From the cold and traveling all day for a month, I got so sick. I had a cold, and I had pain all over my body. For the whole month, I was not able to take a shower. Lice and ticks were everywhere, in my hair all over my body. I was sick inside and out. I started throwing up day and night. I was constantly coughing, which gave me a persistent sore throat; I had never felt that sick before. I started believing that I would never survive to start fighting again. Many in my position would have just requested to be taken home. In fact, many did; nevertheless, I made up my young mind with determination. I had chosen this life. It was not what I expected, but I knew it was for the right cause, so I pushed on. Some days, I felt while I was walking that I was stumbling in a sleepy haze. I could not believe what I was enduring. I truly never thought it was possible that I could be doing this day after day. I had never considered myself especially strong or overly determined; but though I was sick, exhausted, and frustrated, a small part of me was filled with pride that I could just keep going. As the month wore on, fatigue seemed to drain the last of my will. I just wanted to lie down on the ground and relax for a moment even though there was no place to use as a bed. I was so tired; all my body wanted was to collapse. Still, something inside of me wouldn't give up, wouldn't lie down. I finally understood how human beings can find the will to accomplish what they really believe in when their strength and energy are gone. I realized that the only people that really understood me were those same Peshmerga who had that dream of independence. We were together in our suffering and in our goals; nothing would impede us.

Starting out, I was not used to such living conditions. However, as time wore on, my body adjusted to the punishment I was giving it. I got better and stronger, and soon this life was just routine. It didn't get easier to do; it was just easier to endure. However, this soldier's life I had was just the beginning, and real troubles were much worse than these daily inconveniences.

As months went by, I began to realize how, why, and what made us join and suffer like this to become a Peshmerga. I believe the biggest element of my own determination was to see how everyone was so determined to improve the life of the Kurdish people for the better. I remember one of my friends, who was as young as I was, how he was talking about death during the fighting. His name was Hazhar. He believed with surety that bullets could not penetrate him. This conviction remained despite any fierce combat we were engaged in or whether or not our enemy was in a better position. He used to say, "No bullet will penetrate me or kill me." One day, we were in fierce fighting, attacking the enemy position; and a bullet hit him directly in the head. I thought he would never survive. Nevertheless, he somehow survived the wound and was transferred to a hospital in Iran. His injury left him paralyzed, and I didn't see him again for many years.

Years later when I returned to Kurdistan after living in America, I saw him at one of the shops my brother took me to. I didn't recognize the ragged, crippled man pleading for help outside the shop. He was simply another man who was paralyzed and pleading for mercy. My brother asked me, "Do you know this guy was a PUK Peshmerga?" I asked who he was. He told me that his name is Hazhar. After he gave me the description of where he had served in the Peshmerga, I could not believe my eyes! It was the same man who had fought beside me for the Kurdish people and their rights. I recalled with tragic irony how he had said to us that bullets could not penetrate him. It was the same man but only the shell of the confident Peshmerga I had listened to. He seemed so much older. The toll on his body and mind had aged him quickly, and he moved like an old man. It hurt me to see that people were even making fun of him after realizing that this was the same man with whom I had fought alongside as Kurdish Peshmerga forces and seeing now he was no longer the same. That feeling killed me inside, and I could not imagine how hard that would be. Here was a former peshmerga who had risked his life to free his people. He had been paralyzed in that struggle and now was left pleading for someone to assist him because he could not work and his own Kurdish government abandoned him. No one cared to help him survive. My brother told me that Hazhar even has a couple of sisters who are now married but their families could not or would not help him. As a result, he was homeless and went from door to door to survive.

All of that happened years later, of course; but during the time I spent in the Khoshnawati region, I began to realize how hard it was to be in the Peshmerga. The majority of the Kurdish people loved the name—Peshmerga. It filled them, as it had me as a boy, with a secret wonder, with thoughts of honor and gallantry and bravery in battle. However, to be one of them required so many personal sacrifices. Most of the villagers were like my parents. They were more than happy to support and praise the freedom fighters, but they were much less likely to join or send their own sons to join. As a Peshmerga, you trudged endless miles, slept wherever you found shelter, ate when possible, and most importantly, risked your own life for the cause. In spite of these hardships, it was amazing to see so many individuals both old and young have such a high morality to deduct their life for the Kurdish cause and national freedom.

In my time in Khoshnawati, I was never involved in any kind of fighting. Nevertheless, this first excursion was grueling, long, and hard. We hiked endless miles to ensure that our region was secure and that the people were taken care of. It was not something I had expected at all. I had thought we were going to be on daring raids and fierce battles. I came to realize that most of the time, we were just walking. Being a Peshmerga, I realized, was not an easy task. I came back sore and sick from that first assignment. The sickness turned sour, and I thought that I might die without ever seeing combat. I developed a high fever and couldn't keep anything in my stomach. As I was recovering from my sickness, many of my comrades helped me and fed me at our headquarters. It still took me weeks to recover from my flu and then a few more weeks to regain my strength. Finally, after another month, I was well enough to travel. I found out that my friend Karwan (or Faisl), with whom I had journeyed to join the Peshmerga, had left already to join a group in the Koya region. He asked me to join him, and so I asked my commanders if I could join their group. I often sought out these people, my own people, to walk and fight besides because they were from the same village or region as me. We had grown up together, and we were good friends. It was easier to remember why I was sacrificing so much when I was with those who reminded me of my home.

As I was preparing to leave, however, I found out that my older brother Mohammed had rejoined the resistance with the PUK Peshmerga. He was a Peshmerga with a different Kurdish Party: the Communist Party or, in Kurdish, Heezbi Shuhee. He actually came to our base there at Khoshnawati. It was amazing after so many years to see my older brother in the same Peshmerga group I was with, in this case, the PUK Peshmerga. My brother Mohammed had been a member of the Peshmerga for so many years. He has been a member of the PDK, Social Party, Communist Party, etc. Throughout his youth, he was always part of the Kurdish revolution and carried his gun to fight against the Iraqi government. The last time I had seen my brother was in 1983, almost four years before. I was very happy to see him again, so I decided I would postpone my transfer for a few weeks.

Talking with Mohammed, I found out that he had joined the PUK group with a Social Party Peshmerga under the command of a man called Doctor Rashid. He was a very well-known high-ranking official in the resistance. Mohammed was a good friend of Doctor Rashid. He was not a real doctor but a nurse. They called him Doctor because as a younger man, he had been working in Erbil when he got in an argument with government officials who were always butting in and saw how the corrupt government was doing a lot of persecution against any person who showed any resistance to the regime.

He was so fed up with this oppression and corruption that he decided to join the resistance. He stole a whole bunch of medical supplies and medicines from the hospital he was working at. It was rumored that he killed a man and then escaped with the stolen supplies to join the Peshmerga. Mohammed and he were the same age and had been in the resistance for a long time together. Doctor Rashid was very famous in his own right and a well-respected Peshmerga leader and fighter, so when he joined the PUK, he brought many more fighters with him. His exploits, bravery, and intellect were legendary; so it was a huge morale boost for our forces to know that he was with us and had brought so many of his great Peshmerga. It was especially joyful for me since my brother was now fighting with me. Nevertheless, I did not have that much time to enjoy our time together since I was leaving for the Koya District.

Chapter 4

Revolutionary

Moving to the Koya Region

After a few weeks with my brother, I knew that it was time to leave. It was in the late fall of 1986. I left the Khoshnawti region and joined my friends in Koya. At this point in time, I was part of the Kurdish Peshmerga charged with the responsibility of protecting high-ranking persons. In this case, it was Mamosta Bakir. Mamosta Bakir was a tall man with a quiet demeanor. He was very kind and looked out for us as much as possible, especially regarding food and clothes. He rarely talked to us directly; but whenever we had a request, Omer, our team lead, would let him know, and we would soon receive it.

From left (Wasman, Faysal and Dlshad- children are unknown)

Mamosta was his code name; it meant *teacher*. He joined the PUK back in 1979 after graduating from college as a teacher. Many of the Peshmerga used names that referred to their previous lives. This title was appropriate for him as many of the Peshmerga looked to him for guidance. He was also well known within the PUK high command. Mamosta Bakir was commander of the entire Koya region. When I got there, things seemed to be a little bit easier at first. Koya is a flat plateau. I had been used to walking and hiking everywhere. We went up and down through the mountains. It was nice that it was just flat. To add to our ease, we had our own vehicles while we were traveling to different villages with our dignitaries.

We formed a tight group of five from my village: Omer was the team leader. He was a veteran Peshmerga with the PUK. He was actually well known among the PUK leadership and, as such, was wanted and actively hunted by the Iraqi regime. Omer's brother Khalid was a little older than us. He was very quiet and kind. He was so gentle as well. Years after this, he was captured during the Anfal campaign, and as punishment for being a Peshmerga, he was taken high in the air by helicopter and then violently thrown out to his death. We never recovered his body. The fourth member of our group was Faisl (known as Karwan, his Peshmerga pseudonym). He was the boy I ran away with. Finally, there was Wasman, who was also my age and with whom I had played soccer together when we were children.

Mamosta Bakir and Shaheed Rebaz

It was actually very nice to be with these friends from my own village. There were so many memories, events, and people that we could relate to. So much of our time was spent hiding and waiting that it was nice to have people I could really talk to.

There was very little infrastructure in our part of the country. It was already difficult for citizens to contact each other from different areas, and this difficulty was only augmented when you were part of a rebellion. I had heard very little from my family the entire time I had been out. The only news I got was from others from my village who joined the resistance. Travel was also highly restricted. My family lived in a highly government-controlled region, so it was very conspicuous and dangerous for them to simply travel to a known Peshmerga stronghold. One day, to my surprise, Khalid's brother Omer, who was in charge of our team, said, "You and Khalid go to

Hasso's house." We both looked at each other, wondering why. Hasso was one of the well-known men in the village of Kanibi and was very close to the PUK Koya's leadership. It was very strange for two regular Peshmerga to be invited to such an important man's home. When we arrived, Hasso graciously welcome us into his home. As soon as we entered the house, he quickly closed the door and furtively led us to a dark room. Two women were sitting on the floor in our customs. As our eyes adjusted to the light, we could recognize them. It was Khalid's mother and my mother waiting for us. This was the first time I had seen my mother in over a year. They stood up and embraced us. Then they cried, and we started talking. We sat there for a couple of hours, talking about the village and our families. We asked them so many questions about how they are doing. They told us all the news about our neighbors and friends, but most of all, we talked about our family and what was happening with each person. I told about some of my adventures and what things I could talk about. The morning wore on; and our hosts, Hasso's family, prepared lunch for us and kindly fed us while we talked on and on. Finally, it was time for us to return to our duties. As we were leaving, my mother held me firmly in her arms. She looked into my eyes and said, "Your father asked me to kiss you for him. Please give me one last kiss before you go." I kissed her gently on her wet cheek. As we were walking out, she looked at me, like she did when I was a child. "Please be careful, son," she admonished, and we said our final farewells. I didn't see her again for another year and a half.

It was too dangerous to travel during the day, so we hid our vehicles with mud and then moved at night. All during the day, we could hear the airplanes and helicopters flying over while we were hiding. We would hide on the bank of the Greater Zab, the same river that had claimed our friend Ghazim. If we didn't have the riverbank, we would camouflage ourselves with mud and bushes. On rare occasions, we would even be able to hide out in sympathetic homes of the local villages. During the day, we would talk while our commander, Mamosta Bakir, would decide which village or area we would go to next. As commander, he was constantly gathering information. He needed to find out about troop movements and relevant political issues—local, national, and even international. He would also put together information on the social climate and local internal issues. There was really no police force that could be trusted in Iraq, and therefore, community issues and concerns were handled by the locals. When these circumstances were inadequate, we were often relied on to rectify the situations. We would sometimes mediate between villagers, oust spies, hold court, and settle disputes.

A few months later, Mamosta Bakir had us get together because we would be traveling soon. We didn't know where exactly, but he only mentioned that we were going to the Khoshnawaty region. One thing we knew was that we couldn't take our cars because there was no access road from Koya to Khoshnawaty. We were not very excited about the prospect of walking and hiking all the way to the mountains, but who were we to refuse an order? That is what we volunteered for: to fight and be ready whenever and wherever we are needed and are called PUK Peshmerga.

Days before Seri Rash

A few days before the Seri Rash operation, we arrived in the Khoshnawati region (Simaquli), the PUK Hawler headquarters, or the command center (which is called Malband-y Se, "Third Brand of Hawler" in English). At the time, our forces were scattered all over the area and surrounding villages. No one knew what the PUK high-ranking commanders were planning. We knew it had to be something big, since so many of us were stationed in the region.

One of my friends at Simaquli told me that the town of Heeran had been emptied by the Iraqi government. The PUK had an office there. Mamosta Osman, who was a distant relative, and his younger brother, Akram, who was my friend, were both stationed at that village as PUK party representatives. Akram and I were the same age, and we had a lot in common, from friends and family members. I knew that he had joined the PUK force, and now he was a Peshmerga as well. The office had not been affected by the regime, but when I found out he was still there, I wanted to go to see him. After all, I had to do something since we had been told that we would have to wait for a few days in this area. I decided, to kill time, I would visit my friend in Heeran.

The next day in the morning, I told my team leader, Omer, that I was going to Heeran to see my friend. I am not even sure if I had breakfast or not before I left, which would come back to haunt me later. I just started walking and climbing the mountains toward Heeran. The town, I had been told, was just on the other side of the mountains. Someone told me it should not be that far—just a few hours' walking distance. I walked for more than three hours; in the afternoon, I arrived in Heeran. It was relatively vacant as expected, so very few people were there. I asked one of them where the PUK office was. He pointed at the school and said, "Mamosta Osman's office is in there." I walked toward the school and asked someone if Akram was there. The man replied that he was in his room. He led me to him, and the minute Akram saw me, he was surprised and delighted at the same time. We start to hug and kiss each other as we do in our culture. We talked for hours. He provided us lunch, and we continued talking all afternoon. I realized it was getting late and I had to be getting back. Right before sunset, I told him I was going back to Sumaquli.

It was January, which meant that the weather was usually very cold, and in the mountains, it would be freezing and often snow. After I left Heeran, clouds were gathered above me, and it looked like it was going to storm. I had to climb the mountain again, which I wanted to do before it got too dark. I reached the top of the mountain and found a rock, and I sat down on it and turned around to see where I had come from. The view took my breath away. I had been hiking in the mountains for so many months, and before, I was simply a child. I guess I just never really looked at the land and its beauty and never appreciated what our people were fighting for. From my rock, I looked out on the valley over the town of Heeran. I had hiked up above the elevation of the cloud, so from my perspective, I could see the dark underbelly of the storm cloud hanging ominously over the small town, but the light above me turned the cloud white on the top. The surrounding valleys and mountains were awash in color from the last rays of the sunset and seemed almost like a vision. The beauty of the dark cloud over the city of Heeran was so astonishing. After many hours of climbing, I felt so rested. I did not feel any pain or fatigue. Even though it was lightly snowing on the frigid mountaintop, I did not feel cold. Instead, I could feel the fresh air hitting my face, and I drank in deep breaths as though I was drinking fresh water from a mountain stream. It tasted so good. I tried to take as much air as I could. It was the most fantastic moment. I had often thought of the plight of the people of Kurdistan, but now for the first time, I felt the beauty of Kurdistan, and I realized why the Kurds had defiantly held this land for so many centuries and even now why so many young people like me were willing to die for this land. I stayed there transfixed for a quarter of an hour watching the sunset before I came to reality again and looked up at the sky. The cloud that had rested over the town had grown and now engulfed the mountain as well. It was dark and black, and I could tell it was going to bring heavy snow. I said to myself that I had better leave if I had any hope of reaching my destination on time that night.

I started walking in the direction I believed was Samaquli. I think it must have been close to being correct at first, but the small intermittent flakes quickly turned into a mountain blizzard. After an hour or so, the storm was getting so bad, I could not see that far, and I was no longer so sure that I was going in the right direction. I did not realize, though, that I had completely lost my way back to Samaquli. A few hours later trudging through the snow, I was happy to see the lights of another village down below the mountain. I was not sure what the name of the village was, and I was not aware there was another village in this area, but looking down from the top of the hill, I was relieved when I saw the lights because I was getting nervous that I might have to walk all night in the blizzard. I suddenly saw a group of people walking toward me. I asked them where we were and where they were going. They told me, "We are going to Samaquli." I was surprised when they said that. I asked, "Where are you coming from?" They said, "We are coming from Heeran." And they pointed to the light and said, "This is Heeran."

I did not realize I was so lost in the blizzard that I had been walking in circles the whole time around the same area. Basically,

106

after many hours of walking, I had come back to the same place. The only difference was that I was a couple of kilometers away from where I had left the city of Heeran hours before. If I had not gotten their help, I would have had to go back to Heeran thinking I was in Samaquli, or I would have just gotten stuck in the mountains overnight. I thought about how foolish I was that I didn't even ask for directions before I started. I used the small group of people to help me get in the right direction. I felt much better since they were from the area and knew the mountain very well. In a few hours, I arrived in Simaquli. It was such a relief to finally start to thaw out. I decided I would not try to do anything else foolish with this brief time off that would get me killed before I really started fighting.

Seri Rash Operation

When I hear about Seri Rash today, the name brings different images to my mind. As a child, it meant vacation time and spending days on the top of the mountain, enjoying the beautiful view over the city of Erbil. When I became a Peshmerga, it was a nightmare of blood bodies and bullets in a dark night assaulting Saddam's cabins. Try to imagine a vacation retreat of skiing and relaxation as a child in Park City, Utah, for a weekend and then later having to storm those same ski resorts that had become military compounds. It was like taking a ripping apart a beautiful memory and leaving the shredding pieces to lie in ruins in my mind.

Dr. Bewar, with a group of Peshmerga standing first on
the right. Kareem is sitting the first one on the left.

This brief reprieve from traveling all over, however, lasted only a month or two. Word came down that something big was going to happen. We started preparations for another big operation without really knowing what it was going to be. It was a little exciting, to tell the truth, but we were also a little anxious. When we actually found out what it was, our excitement and anxiety were amplified; we were all both terrified and giddy with excitement. We were going to attack Seri Rash! This was an Iraqi military base at the top of the Seri-Rash Mountain.

Dr. Bewar with a couple of his Peshmerga
friends. He is standing in the middle

We were going to be part of one of the biggest operations carried out by our PUK Peshmerga force against the Iraqi military to date. Our entire division, about 150 men, was called to this operation. Our commander, of course, was able to travel in a vehicle, but the rest of us had to walk. It took us several hours to hike to the base of the mountain we would be attacking. It was January of 1987, so we had to wait at the base of the mountain in bitterly cold weather. Often, it would rain and then turn to snow, making it all a cold muddy hole. The wet, cold weather made preparations and movements uncomfortable and difficult, especially now that so many troops were converging to our base. Over one thousand Peshmerga gathered in the Khoshnawati region to attack Seri Rash. We did our best to travel in small groups in order to not draw too much attention to our convergence. The Iraqi regime might have had an idea about the mass Peshmerga movement, but I am sure they did not know where the Peshmerga were planning to attack.

Finally, the time came. However, miserable it was at the bottom of the mountain, it just kept getting worse the higher we climbed. Toward the top of the mountain, it was such a blizzard we were not able to see anything. We walked for hours to get to our location of attacks. That march up the mountain is frozen in my mind forever. It's important to remember that we did not have clothing fit for such weather. Our shoes were literally made of plastic. They came from Iran, and they were in the shape of a boot, but I believe that bare feet would have been more comfortable and less cold than wearing those miserable coverings. We didn't have winter coats or warm leggings. We didn't even have gloves. In fact, we actually were anxious to start shooting because we could then warm our hands on the heat from the gun barrels. We did wear our traditional Kurdish turban, which was actually the best part of our clothing since it covered our heads and ears, and could be pulled in front to cover our faces. We were wet and frozen. Our hands, feet, and faces were numb while we continued through the driving wet snow.

This operation was commanded and undertaken by one of the best-known Kurdish leaders in Kurdistan, Kosrat Ali. He is well known by the name of Kak Kosrat, which means in English "Mr. Kosrat," a title that showed respect and honor. He was a famous Kurdish PUK member and was loved and admired by the Peshmerga and Kurds in general. His courage and leadership style were amazing to me and many of my comrades. He was such a brave and valiant fighter; I will never forget how he demonstrated true leadership to those he commanded. Throughout the whole operation, he never backed down or retreated one step. He always fought in front of his charge: leading them. That act alone inspired the men that saw him. His bravery was unquestioned, and his leadership was unchallenged. He loved his people and would fight alongside the lowest-ranking Peshmerga, knowing the risk they were in, knowing he had commanded them and was willing to put his own life at risk to bolster his troops and ensure that such a massive operation, so carefully mapped out, would be successful.

Eventually, we overpowered the Iraqi guards and destroyed their positions. Reports circulated that over twenty of our brave comrades were martyred in the operation. Unfortunately, there was no time for celebration. Directly after taking all the positions away from the Iraqi military, we were ordered to leave and return to our safe area. We knew that the Iraqi military was still much stronger. We had been lucky that they were not as secure or organized in that region and thus had won a quick victory, but they would come with massive troops and air support. We also highly suspected that Saddam's forces would use chemical weapons on us as he had in other regions we had heard about. We didn't even dare to spend the night in our conquered territory. As a result, hungry, tired, and still freezing on the top of the snow-blown mountain, we abandoned the military bases we had just liberated. Thinking back, I am not sure that abandoning Seri Rash was a good strategic decision. However, I was positive about Kak Kosrat when he made such a decision. There was a reason behind it. There was a rumor at the time Kak Korsat made the decision because he was afraid the Iraqi regime would attack us with the chemicals and he did not want to lose more Peshmerga. Leaving Seri Rash, therefore, seemed the best option even though our force was tired, hungry, and cold.

The fierce fighting, fear, and stress had left our bodies sweating and used. Now trudging through the piling snow in sweat-soaked clothing in shoes not fit for winter and so tired the marrow in our bones seemed to ache, we made our way silently and grudgingly back down the treacherous slopes. All through that night, we marched. My friend Kareem was walking next to me, quickly plodding along. His footfalls started to slow, and his breathing grew weak. He turned to me and almost pleadingly told me that he needed to sit down for just a minute or so. I urged him to walk a little farther and find shelter to build a fire or something. He dismissed my idea and said he only needed a minute to catch his breath and then he would catch up with me and we would return to camp. I begged him to not sit in the snow. It was too cold. We had to find shelter. He calmly sat down on the soft snow, and his whole body seemed to relax. He smiled faintly and told me that he would only be a moment, and then he would catch up. I could do nothing else, as I was starting to freeze, and the snow was looking more and more inviting. I admonished him one more time that he should get up quickly and I would wait for him. He waved me on with a smile. I moved on alone while he was swallowed up in the snowstorm. I walked on for another half hour when I saw a small building. It was packed with Peshmerga who were all crowded into this small one bedroom. They had a fire in there that had filled the room with smoke, but they didn't care, and I didn't care. I wormed my way in as well just to warm my fingers a little bit. It was early morning when I finally felt a little more energy. I left, knowing I had to keep moving. This feeling of needing to keep moving saved my life then and many other times. I eventually crossed paths with a truck that was driving around to pick up soldiers. They drove me into the village where there was a small mosque. It had a propane heater in the center of the room, and men were standing or lying around trying to thaw out. The worst cases were brought in and left to hopefully survive.

As I was starting to get feeling back in my toes and face, much later in the morning. I saw my friend Kareem being carried into the mosque. I walked over to him, and he looked like a frozen corpse. Somehow, however, he was still alive. The cold weather, however, had hit him so badly. It was like he had a heart attack. He eventually made a full recovery; but many Peshmerga in our unit, especially those wounded in the operation, succumbed to the frozen mountain and died on their way back to safety. Two more of my friends from our Koya division, already suffering from their wounds, died from the cold weather. However, Kareem made it and survived and luckily didn't have to have any amputations like so many of the others.

Suddenly, out of nowhere came a figure I would never have expected and a voice that I will never forget. I can see the whole scene even today; I was walking through the headquarters when suddenly an excited voice jolted me from my grim and somber reverie. My older brother Mohammed was suddenly and impossibly hugging me and kissing my cheek. "Great! You are alive. You made it." He said to me, "I thought you would never be able to make it in such harsh cold weather in addition to fighting." When I saw him, he was very happy but did not show that much emotion. That was his personality. He is a very strong person, and as an older brother, that is what I expected from Mohammed.

In spite of the fact that we had abandoned our dearly fought positions and seemingly had to retreat in the moment of victory, the operation was very successful. At that time, Monte Carlo, the Arabic French radio and one of the biggest broadcasters in the Middle East, reported on the operation in Siri Rash. Up until then, very little of our resistance made it into actual news. We had felt so isolated from the rest of the world. It had always seemed that we were invisible to the great powers of the world, and our feeble attempts at self-governance were unnoticed by the rest of humanity. That announcement on public radio airways by itself, in the eyes and minds of the PUK leadership and the Kurdish people, was an indication of our success and recognition for all the Kurdish people as well. It was also a personal insult to Saddam since the operation location was very wide and the many cabins that were built there had been nicknamed "Saddam's house." It meant that the rest of the Middle East and not just Iraq now saw that the Iraqi military was not as strong as they claimed and that Kurdish resistance could make an impact on the regime.

Our mourning for the fallen and celebration of the victory quickly faded as we were ordered to move to another region, Sulaimania. Our victory had emboldened our leaders, and we were told that much bigger fighting would take place. My short-lived stint in comfortable transportation officially ended, so once again we had to start walking for days to another region. Though it was not as cold as hiking the mountain of Siri Rash it was still wintertime, and we had to trudge through freezing muddy roads, traveling for weeks to get to our position in the Sergalu and Bergalu where the PUK headquarters were located. Talabani, the head of the PUK house, was there along with many politburo members. I was excited to go and see the region where PUK leaders are located. Also, the name of these two villages is well known to us, but for me, I did not know what it looked like.

Now Seri Rash is no longer a public place for Kurds and Iraqis to vacation and enjoy the beautiful views. It is controlled by the

Kurdish Barzani family, and no one is allowed to visit or go near this area.

The Epic of Liberation

It was about February of 1987 when all the Peshmerga forces from all the regions were requested to mobilize to the Sulaimania region for an operation. We were also moved to join all PUK forces. It was the biggest PUK operation carried out in modern Kurdish history against the Iraqi military. The vast area targeted was hundreds of miles wide. Our group was charged with the responsibility of taking the Gojar Mountain post, which was the highest peak in the area. Just looking up at the mountain, nightmares of the attack on Siri Rash seemed to stiffen my joints and cause my bones to ache. The mountain position was critical to our operation. As with Siri Rash, the highest peaks allowed for the most surveyance. If we could take out the military's vision, we could blind them to our subsequent attacks.

We waited for weeks on the valley floor, expecting the order to march at any time. The valley was cold and empty. There was little food in the camp as our supply lines were insufficient to provide for such a contingent of fighters. Especially since our food was donated primarily by local villages amiable to our cause. We did have some support for outside rations and supplies. I remember we had some sleeping bags to use at night. But the sleep bags were very limited, and not all of us had one. At the time, I didn't care where the supplies came from; anything we got was a welcome blessing. Later on, however, I realized the operation was being supported by the Iranian regime. Even our sleeping bags were provided by the Iranian military, an arrangement made previously by the head of the PUK secretary, Mr. Talabani. The Iranians had their own plans and purposes in supporting us, but like I said any gift was welcome.

Our mission was simple: take the mountaintop and retreat. This would be just like Siri Rash. I was in a secondary support battalion. We were to follow the initial strike force which was charged with breaking through the security forces, and we were to follow with additional support if needed, then strip the facility of any useful material and make a victorious retreat. We were filled with the nervous energy that accompanies danger and violence.

It wasn't until April that we finally began the campaign. I had hoped that the spring would have been stronger and that it wouldn't have been so damned cold. However, it was still frigid on our march up the slopes through the mountain roads that were still covered with deep snow. The wind tore at our jackets and stung our cold, exposed faces. It stole my breath away countless times, and I would have to stop and gulp frozen air as though I had been drowning. The defense at the top of the mountain was minimal, and the first wave soon overpowered the soldiers, and their position was taken by our force. By the time our group arrived, the fighting had subsided. We ransacked through the compounds, emptying its stores of weapons and munitions. We made a great haul, but then we received word that instead of a hasty retreat, we were ordered to sit tight and maintain our position. Apparently, our commanders had decided that they were tired of giving back conquered ground. This news came as a shock. We were proud of our victory and holding the land felt good, but we knew our forces were undersupplied, outmanned, and outgunned. Holding this position for any significant amount of time would take everything we had, and we already had very little.

But now we had to maintain our position. At the beginning of the operation, we had lost a couple of brave Peshmerga. As the hours dragged on and night came, we realized that holding this position would probably take more than we had and perhaps our lives as well. The Iraqi military special force soon began an unending assault to take the mountain back. They were supported by helicopters, fighter jets, and a seemingly unending bombardment of mortars and rockets as well. Day after day dragged on; one by one our forces were reduced as man after brave man was martyred for their land. We were not true soldiers. We didn't have actual military training; we never marched in formation. We were a ragtag group of boys, farmers, shop owners, and ranchers. We didn't understand military tactics or firing positions or hardly anything. Only our commanders had any tactical knowledge. Some of them were very skilled in the art of war. But for the main forces, our main weapon was bravery, and usually, it was foolhardy at that. Our commanders fought at our heads. They were the first in combat and the last to retreat. We followed them like children after superheroes. Even they, however, took foolish risks and made costly mistakes.

We fought on stubbornly through freezing temperatures, near starvations, and low munitions. The head of our unit—a small, unobtrusive, yet inspiring man named Ali Masifi—led us. He was the same commander that was in charge of the region when I had first joined. As was his nature, he fought as though he was invincible. It was part of his inspiration to his men to stand in full view of the enemy in defiance of their firepower. He had been using a Russian RPG to stop a new wave from the Iraqi military out in the open and was fully exposed when he was struck by a bullet from a sniper. He died only a few moments after he was hit. Word of his death spread over the mountaintop like wildfire. Our resolve seemed to freeze like our toes in our boots. In our hearts, we knew it was over. Our minds and bodies took a little more convincing.

We stubbornly continued fighting, but this tragic event affected each of our morale. The excitement, confidence, and bravado that had filled our breasts when we took the mountain had shrunk inside us. We were tired, hungry, and bitterly cold. The unending onslaught of the might of the military seemed to crush us into the frozen mountain dirt. We were ants to this regime. All we had were some AK-47s, which were most likely stolen or captured. We were without proper uniforms, enough supplies, backup, and hope of reinforcements. How we had resisted for so many days the special forces with their advanced weaponry, skilled soldiers, and actual food was a miracle in itself. The only way, I believe, I and so many of my comrades had continued to stand and fight for as long as we had was because we knew the reason we were doing this; we were convinced that our cause was just because of the history of our Kurdish struggle and the belief we had rights to fight our enemy. We believed that it was a matter of survival to maintain our culture, heritage, and identity. There was no other choice for us. We had to fight, and we were zealots in the cause. Our enemy, on the other hand, was more mercenary than anything. They were forced to join by the regime. Some of them were even Kurds pressed into service. They had no joy in serving, and many had no real loyalty to Saddam.

Regardless of our fervent resistance and our zealous convictions, our defeat was inevitable. Word soon came for us to abandon the Gojar Mountain post. We gathered the arms and munitions we had captured and began the treacherous climb back down the snow-covered mountain. Most of us were so tired and hungry that we barely could walk. There was no logistic support of any kind to get food and have warmer clothes to wear. At the top, we had maybe one or two sleeping bags per twenty men. We rested in turns and shared the bag between us. That meant we had not had a full night's rest in over a week. Our food had been just as limited. My group had been the backup for the operation. There was no one else to follow us. We had not planned on staying on the top and, therefore, no plans had been made to send in supplies.

I do recall hearing about some of the members of the Iranian intelligence that were providing targeting positions at the top of the mountain as eyes and ears to our limited cannons to target the Iraqi military. However, such logistical aid was very limited. Besides, the Iranian government did not care about the Kurdish people or their rights. They used us for their own political agenda as they have done always throughout the history of the region.

As I was walking down with our group, I saw Peshmerga everywhere, like ants fleeing a burning log in a fire, withdrawing from their positions and moving down to the unknown retreat position. The fighting only intensified as we abandoned post after post. I saw many of our comrades killed (martyred) within that short period of time. The scene was devastating as I was looking up and down the mountains. It was a heartbreaking scene of the lifeless bodies of our brave Peshmerga killed during the operation. Mules and horses were laden with the bodies of our fallen comrades. The blood ran down the sides of the beasts and down their legs, leaving dark-stained snowy hoof tracks, which we followed in our exhausted and tragic retreat. This visage of death and misery will haunt my dreams and memories as long as I live. There are really no words to describe the aching I felt both physically, mentally, and spiritually.

Most of these bodies were solemnly and secretly buried somewhere, god knows where! Their mothers, fathers, sisters, or brothers will never be able to see their loved ones again, dead or alive. Such tragic deaths were only punctuated by the fact that there could be no funeral ever held for these heroes. After all, if the Iraqi government intelligence agency, the Mukhabarat, were to find families having a funeral for a member of the Peshmerga, they would charge them with treason. Such a thing was forbidden to take place. Families were not even allowed to mourn when they actually found out. Any mention of the deeds and bravery of a rebel meant imprisonment at best and at worst death and destruction for the whole family and perhaps the whole village where the youth came from. What always hurt me the most, though, was the thought that these heroes who sacrificed their lives for the Kurdish cause would never enjoy their youth. They had been robbed, as I had been, of an innocent and happy childhood. They had been pushed beyond the limits of what humans should be forced to endure. They had seen atrocities and had sacrificed their lives as human beings free to choose and be with their families for a shortened manhood and a shallow unmarked grave. Such injustice in this world nearly drove me mad with anger and frustration.

As we walked the trail of retreating, the Peshmerga from the Democratic Party of Iran stood flanking both sides of the road. They were from Iran and another political party, so they could not join us in the fight. But secretly, they knew we were their brothers; so they handed out water, food, and whatever supplies they could to us while we walked by. There are many divisions among the Kurds politically, but at heart, we are all still one people. That was shown by the apparent betrayal by these men, who had been supported by the Iraqi government to disrupt the Iranian government. They were truly courageous and loyal to Kurdistan.

After our retreat, we went into hiding in some safer mountains. We finally could look forward to some actual rest, perhaps some food. Soon after setting up a secret camp, we got a goat. One of our members butchered it and set about cooking it for our small group.

We all pitched in to help as well; however, there was not much to do. We went through our packs looking for any remnants of supplies we could find. There was nothing. We did not have anything else to eat: no bread, no rice, nothing green and healthy. The only item we finally found was a little canned tomato paste which we mixed with the meat while it cooked. It was very tough and tasted horrible. In fact, even though we were quite literally starving, it was still difficult to force the meat down. I was able to force it down, but unfortunately, I got food poisoning. This experience was going from bad to worse to terrible. For days, I could not eat anything else. However, rations did eventually arrive. I remained deathly ill. I couldn't keep anything down and started losing weight. I got so skinny many of my comrades expected me to die. To this day, I don't know why I did not die. I remember I joked in my sickened, starved state, "What a shame. I was not martyred in the fighting, but now I am dying of food poisoning." I eventually overcame the sickness, though, and started getting better. It took me several weeks, but I put weight on again and soon started feeling like I would survive. When I was well enough, my comrades and I finally were able to pack up and leave our makeshift hideout. We put our packs back on, pulled on our plastic boots, and trudged onto a different area.

After Epic Operation

Even though we had withdrawn to another location and it was already a couple of weeks after our victory and retreat, we could still hear bombing activity from the Iraqi army. There was shooting everywhere, especially in areas that were close to where the Iraqi government was still attacking the liberated mountain locations. Nevertheless, the fighting was actually taking place in every direction. It seemed that we had touched a torch to a spark that had ignited the entire region. Roads, villages, mountains, and valleys were now all vulnerable to the wrath of the Iraqi military. Worse, whereas before they had been an overwhelming force with their powerful yet conventional firepower, they now added a more deadly and atrocious weapon—one that altered our entire mode of attack and defense. It also both enraged and terrified the general populace of Kurdistan. We could no longer simply hide in bunkers, in caves, or behind walls to hide from the bombardment of RPGs, tanks, or planes. The Iraqi government started using chemical bombs against the Peshmerga and often on civilians as well. There were countless stories of our brave Peshmerga forces that hid in bunkers, only to be poisoned and tortured by the chemicals that ravaged their bodies and lungs until they died in agony. Civilians—mothers who were used to sheltering their children by hiding in their homes until the attacks had passed, often with the elderly and infirm—would be found dead with tortured looks on their innocent faces from the horrendous effects of these gasses. They had thought they were safe in their homes, but now Saddam could reach into their most private sanctuaries and kill them indiscriminately simply because they were Kurds.

We continued moving from village to village in attempts to avoid capture, find food, and still continue fighting. In one village in the mountain, there was an unexploded cannon shell. The whole region had been bombarded with chemical weapons so much that we all assumed it was a chemical bomb. We had an expert with us that had already been part of a chemical attack, and he had warned us not to get near it. It was insane that we marched right past a chemical bomb. It was right next to us. We were advised not to touch it. We even stayed in the area for another couple of weeks.

The Perilous Return of the Sleeping Bags

It never ceases to amaze me how different life and culture are in the United States compared with my native land. Traveling here in particular is so much easier, faster, and usually safer. With relatively recent changes in technology, such as cell phones with GPS and maps, it is rare that people need help or get lost on their way to a destination. In my youth back in Kurdistan, people usually asked other people for directions to get around. After living in the United States for a few years and getting to know the culture, I came to realize that it makes for very uncomfortable situations to stop and ask a stranger for directions. I remember when I was living in California a few years ago, I was out with a fellow immigrant, and we were lost. He stopped the car and went up to a stranger to ask for directions. The man stood looking at us strangely. Though he gave us the directions, I'm sure he was thinking, "Wow! Weirdos. Don't they know they have maps and GPS on their phones?" I shrank down in my seat, and when we started driving again, I explained that Americans do not usually talk with strangers to get help. Most use GPS or even an atlas before they have to ask for assistance.

In Kurdistan, the streets, roads, and paths were not as organized as those in America. They have existed for thousands of years in some instances. They have been trodden by so many people and named and renamed, forgotten and remade that it is nearly impossible to know the actual name of a road or if it still exists. Because of this, you always had to talk with the local townspeople to find out how to navigate their land. Since many of the roads were just dirt paths, people rarely told you the street names to turn on. Instead, they used landmarks, abandoned machinery, interesting buildings, and other descriptors to guide travelers on their way.

"Go straight along this road until you come to the edge of the field, where there is an old abandoned plow. Turn right, and follow it until you come to a small river that cuts across the road. There is a bridge that you can cross, and then you will turn again at an old gnarled tree. You will come to a small village, and the person you are looking for lives in the small house with three black goats that feed outside."

Often you would have to ask several people all along the way until you arrived. Everyone asked everyone else how to get places, and it was common and expected of strangers to help each other, unless the people were scared of government problems.

Even though we were fighting for the freedom of our people, the relationship we had with many of the citizens often became strained due to the constant attacks, retaliations, expected supplies, and betrayals. One incident that happened to me in this area made this especially clear to my young mind.

Mamosta Bakir, the head of our unit, asked me to return some equipment to another village. I was told to take a horse and transfer four or five sleeping bags to another region to the Chinar Village, which would take more than a day to get there. Sleeping bags were such a rare commodity for us, and I knew we would miss them, but Bakir explained that Mr. Talabani had asked for them specifically, so we couldn't keep any of them at all.

It was late afternoon by the time I was given a horse and was told that I should leave at once. I did not know the area nor how to get to Chinar at all. I had only been to that village once for a couple of days. To make matters worse, we had moved into the village at night, and we had left in the night as well. I could not remember anything except the general direction. One of my comrades gave a garbled description of the roads and where to go. That was it! I was on my way alone in the late afternoon with the sun already sinking into the horizon on forsaken roads in a war-torn region of nowhere to my intended destination, delivering sleeping bags of all things! To say that I was scared was a major understatement. Soon it was dark, and the night had closed in around me. Here I was, a young rebel fighter traveling in, hopefully, the right direction on a borrowed horse and bereft of my senses—hungry, thirsty, tired, and, most likely, lost— lost but, for my dogged determination, hoping that I was going the right way.

By following the roads, I knew I would eventually arrive somewhere, and I did. I arrived at a sleepy village named Se Kani. It was very dark about an hour or so past sundown. I was dirty, thirsty, hungry, and exhausted. Not to mention, my nerves were fried from watching every shadow and jerking my head at every sound. It was with considerable relief then that I rode into a Kurdish village.

My relief quickly turned to wariness and desperation. The whole village was eerily quiet. There were no lights in the homes, no animals braying. There were no muffled voices from behind cozy homes. All the signs of a living town were gone. There were obvious signs of struggles. The telltale signs of military skirmishes were there, but there was nothing beyond what was normal for most villages I had been to. I was suddenly more scared.

I was lost, I knew, and finally admitted it to myself. I was badly in need of food and water, and I was getting dizzy with fatigue. Being young and not knowing what to do, I remembered that I had something in the way of making a lot of noise to try to get someone's attention. I aimed my AK-47 in the air and started shooting random bursts into the sky to alert someone, anyone, to come and help me.

Unbeknownst to me, this particular village had seen more than its fair share of violence. To compound their plight, they had also had a personal run-in with a group of Kurdish traitors who had abandoned their people and culture and were working for the Iraqi military intelligence. They didn't know whom they could trust. They had no idea if a stranger was simply a hungry traveler or if they were there to kill, gather intelligence, or betray them again. They could not even trust their own people. For this reason, the people of the village had built a secret temporary shelter in the foothills outside the village where they could take refuge quickly to be safe from bombardment, chemical weapons, or betrayal that they assumed was coming again. I had inadvertently set off their defensive protocols. A lone, armed rider dressed as a poor rebel riding into town on a horse had sent them all into a frenzy. They had gathered up everyone and moved them into the hidden shelters while the men had hidden close by with their rifles ready in case of a surprise attack. And so, when I arrived, the whole village was empty but brooding with the air of some mysterious catastrophe. This was when I started firing into the air—a sure sign to them that I was up to no good. My stupidity and desperation almost cost me my life.

Without me knowing, a terrible struggle was going on. Many of the men were about to shoot me simply because I was obviously a threat. Fortunately, cool heads won out. After a few moments, I heard voices from all around me, "Who are you?" I looked around but could see no one. Nor could I tell which direction the voices had come from. "What are you doing here?" the voices demanded. I replied in a strained, anxious voice, "I am Peshmerga. I need to rest, get some food, and also, I need directions." I wearily put away my weapon, knowing that I was surrounded, and waited. After a minute or two, men emerged from the shadows all around me. They were all heavily armed.

One of them approached me, saying, "What unit are you with?"

I told him where I had come from and what I was doing there. He shook his head. "You are fortunate we did not kill you!"

I pleaded, "I have been to this village before, and I know that I have seen people here, but where are all the families? What happened here?" I was told that sometimes the families leave the village to live in the mountains. The man was careful not to say where or even indicate with his eyes. They were still very wary of me.

I learned later about the plight of that particular village and how closely I had come to being shot on sight. That night, however, I stayed there, and they gave me some food. They put a blanket outside by me with a little pillow and let me sleep there. My thoughts were still racing on how close I had come to dying while my body ached to sleep. I am not sure how long it took to fall asleep; however, I know that it was suddenly getting light out. When I got up the next morning, I was given a cup of tea and some bread along with Kurdish yogurt. They gave me directions to the Chinar Village. I graciously thanked them, I believe as much for still being alive as for the hospitality. Then I mounted the borrowed horse and left.

While I was riding my horse much later, I checked my AK-47. I was surprised to see that it had been put on safety. It was not ready to fire, and I realized that even after giving me food and a blanket, they still did not trust me. Somehow, when I was sleeping, they must have snuck up and taken my gun and put the safety on. They were not going to take any chances with me or anyone else, for that matter.

I rode the horse through another mountain until I arrived at my destination. It was about noon when I arrived there, and I gave them to the person I was supposed to deliver them to. After that, it was much easier to get back to my company. When I rode through the town, however, it was empty again, but I was more careful this time to keep my gun tucked away, and I rode quickly through the houses and out of that region. It was late at night when I got back to my temporary location and told my friends what had happened to me during my trip. We had a good laugh, and they told me how happy they were that I had not been killed for my stupidity. Though I laughed with them, my laughter was strained as the incident still sat in my mind like a wound that continued to hurt long after it should have healed. After another week or so, we were told that we were going back to our region, Koya. Therefore, we packed up and started walking again, back through the same route we had taken months ago.

A Loaf of Bread

Often, I think about the way I procured food as a Peshmerga. I feel ashamed of how I was basically begging for food and shelter. Living in the United States, people who go up to strangers asking for food are often stigmatized and ostracized from society. It is assumed that they are homeless with all the implications that the term carries. I have thought about what it would feel like if I were to ask Americans to give me food and a place to sleep, and I cannot imagine the shame I would feel! Well, my situation was totally different. It was expected to do what we had to do to survive so we could continue our resistance.

Throughout my years of service in the mountains, I never remember seeing any Peshmerga carry food with them when they had to travel for long distances. At least not enough food for the trip they would take. If they did have food, it was usually just something simple that they could carry if they had been offered it. Me, I never really thought about it. It was just not that unusual of a phenomenon. I believe that it was because the townspeople were always there to support us. When we needed meals while traveling, it was the normal custom to be asked into a home to eat and even sleep if necessary. I was so used to it that I simply took it for granted: since I was fighting for our people, they were happy and able to provide for me when I got hungry.

One event changed that perspective forever. As we were traveling, I found myself traveling alone for a few hours. It was customary not to travel in large groups. It was a security measure to make us less of a target. I was a growing young man, so I got very hungry. We were passing through another no-name village, like so many others. On the way, I saw an older woman who was baking bread. She could have been any grandmother in the region. They all started to look the same to me. She was no different, though her bread smelled delicious. When I smelled the baking bread, it was very tempting. Without thinking much about it, I decided to go ahead and ask her for some of her bread. When I approached her and asked for the bread, for some reason, she became irate. She snapped, "No!" Then in her Kurdish dialect, she said something that would equate to "Get the hell out of here!"

Shocked, I stood staring, my jaw open, without a word to say. Then I closed my mouth and started walking away from the village. I was walking crestfallen for a minute or two when I heard someone yelling at me. Suddenly wary, I turned around. I saw the same old woman hurrying toward me and calling for me to stop. She was carrying bread in one hand, and in the other was the Kurdish yogurt soda.

I stopped and then took a few steps forward until she was near enough to me. Slightly out of breath, she explained, "I am sorry, my son. I didn't mean to yell at you and say such a cruel thing to hurt you. It just has been very hard for us to be able to feed everyone that walks through our village." She motioned up and down the street as though to show how many people traveled it. "As you know, where we are located, we are seeing so many, and they are all asking for food." Her eyes found mine, and she pleaded, "There is no way we can support such a burden. As you know, how expensive flour is to get up here."

I told her that I did understand. I explained that I was very sorry to have put that guilt on her but that I had not been able to eat all day. With a sympathetic smile, she prodded the warm bread into my hands and the cup of yogurt soda as well. "God be with you," she blessed me and then walked back to her humble home.

I continued walking. The bread tasted so good, but it was mixed now with the salty taste of my tears. I was not mad at her at all. Even when she refused me food, I wasn't angry. My thoughts strayed to all the mothers and grandmothers who handed me a bowl of soup meant for their child or a loaf of bread for their working husbands, as well as the many times I had slept in a stranger's home and they had called me son and treated me as a brother. I could see that her house was located along one of the common routes that the Peshmerga constantly traveled.

These people, the Kurds, my people, were feeding and sheltering us day and night. The toll on them must have been tremendous. Yes, I realized, I was risking my life to save my people, and there were many other Peshmerga who had sacrificed their lives for our people, but these stalwart villagers also sacrificed their lives for us. They were just as tired of the conflict that carried on month after month, weeks on end, daily, hour by hour, and from minute to minute. Their lives were in just as much peril as my own. Food was not easy to get in these areas under the Kurdish Peshmerga control, and it was expensive as well. They had no outside support and had to subsist on what they could grow or trade for.

Still, they gave until it hurt. And when they had given too much like this blessed woman and snapped at a hungry boy, they still found it in their hearts to give even more. I will always be grateful for what these people did for our culture and nation and especially how they helped the Peshmerga throughout the history of our national struggle. If it were not for them, the Kurdish opposition would not have had a chance to survive at all. These people were the heart and soul of the Kurdish revolution then and throughout our past. There is no doubt in my mind all of Kurdistan owes them for the essential service that they provided for the Kurdish rebellion and revolution.

Anfal Campaign

Often, I ask myself why people around the world fight one another. This has been a lifelong question because war and conflict seem to be the only thing I ever saw when two cultures came together, whether it was Iraqi soldiers oppressing the Kurds or Kurdish factions fighting each other. This was especially true in the early 1970s, during the Kurdish revolution, and later on when the 1980 Iraq-Iran War started. I was thinking then, as I often do now, when is the fighting going to stop! Based on my experiences and those of the people around me, we seem to just accept that the fighting will never stop in this region. Unfortunately, throughout history, war and turmoil have always ravaged this region. It has always been the case.

Never was conflict more prominent in my life, though, than in this time period. In the early months of 1988, the Iraqi regime initiated a terrible operation against the Kurds especially, but it included any opposition forces to Saddam's rule. He called this "Anfal." The campaign had actually started a little bit earlier but was now heightened because Saddam knew that the Iraq-Iran War, an eight-year conflict, was coming to an end. Now he could focus his full attention on the rebels in the north. He wanted to make sure that the whole Kurdish nation would pay for what the Kurdish revolution had done against his Iraqi regime. He further knew that the Iranians would no longer be supporting our cause with aid and ammunition, so he felt secure in his retaliation.

In a bold move meant to disgrace his enemies and embolden and justify his supporters' actions, he named the campaign "Anfal." This was a term taken out of context from the Qur'an. In its basic form, the term implies "spoils" or "looting." The usage in the holy book was that soldiers fighting for the cause of Allah against infidels had the right to take anything that they conquered, including animals, grains, money, and even women or slaves. This was a calculated move by Saddam to encourage those who would be attacking the Kurdish villages because it meant they could do whatever they wanted and take whatever they wanted from their conquests. All this were in the name of Islam, even though the Kurds were, for the most part, Muslims and, therefore, the laws of Anfal would not apply. Nevertheless, the actual meaning was distorted to serve his political and vengeful ends.

The ultimate goal of this campaign was to utterly destroy villages and towns that were considered to support the Kurdish opposition. Basically, this included any Kurdish town. The regime recognized that these villages and towns were the heart and soul of the Peshmerga. More than that, they were the means whereby the resistance was sustained. They provided the resources: food; clothing; finances to continue the resistance; and the inspiration for the fighters since they were the mothers, fathers, brothers, sisters, and culture that drove us, the Peshmerga, on in our most desperate fights.

The atrocities and crimes committed by the military during this time cannot be overexaggerated. Though this practice of destruction against the Kurdish people had been practiced for generations throughout our history, Saddam's regime nearly succeeded in wiping Iraqi Kurds off his map. There were many villages that were razed to the dust. The people were beaten, scattered, and arrested. In many circumstances, the regime even used chemical weapons. My own village became an example of this desolation, though no chemicals were used. From late '87 till early '88 in Peerdawood, my home village was completely destroyed. The homes were smashed and scattered, the fields torn up, the animals taken or slaughtered, and even the mosque was demolished in a common yet ironic display of how this was not a true holy war. Even though our village was not a security threat to the government because it could not hide anyone well nor give tactical or financial aid, as it was on the main road and thus highly monitored, it was, nonetheless, destroyed in fulfillment of the Iraqi plan to demoralize and cut off the support to the Peshmerga.

The intensification of the Anfal campaign had several terrible effects due to its increased pressure fueled by greedy policies that encouraged horrendous acts of inhumanity. For instance, for the soldiers and those who participated in the operation, whatever they found, they could loot. This became a huge temptation for the common Iraqi soldier, which was bad enough. But it also had an effect on the Kurds who were scared for their own survival, unsure of the virtues of the Kurdish cause, or simply dishonorable scum who preyed on innocents. Many of these people became traitors to their own families and neighbors. These Kurds were scorned by most and labeled *jash*, which means "little jackass." However, to the regime, they were treated as heroes. It was decreed that they were allowed into every town, every home, and every business. There was no such thing as a right to privacy in our country. Those with knowledge of the people, countryside, and culture were used extensively. Resistance was punished immediately with arrests, burnings, and even death. During this reign of terror known as the Anfal campaign, more than two hundred thousand Kurdish people were detained. These mainly included noncombatants: shopkeepers, mothers, grandparents, and young children.

They were dragged from their homes and villages and never seen or heard from again. At the time, it was suspected and rumored that they were killed and buried in unmarked graves. Only after the conflicts had ended and Saddam had fallen did they start to find these mass graves. Even today, mass graves are being discovered, and the bodies of the forgotten innocents are finally remembered and mourned.

As I have stated, the Peshmerga were a ragtag group of teenagers, shopkeepers, and idealists. We were not trained militias. There were few of the commanders who had a deep understanding or experience in strategy and military maneuvers. The Iraqi military leadership, on the other hand, was educated and trained in the art of war and had better equipment and resources. During the Anfal campaign, we did our best to keep a free and independent district in the north. We strove to protect those villages and towns that had supported us and fought tirelessly to protect the people who had given so much and were in such terrible danger. However, the Iraqis used our passion and inexperience against us. They would often position obvious targets away from the villages on the southern border to draw our forces deeper into the country and away from the unprotected villages. Then while we were fighting or attacking the decoy, they would move with their main forces against the unprotected citizens. It was frustrating work, and we became both demoralized in our hopes but more determined at the same time due to the pure inhumanity of the actions. Fighting the army was unfair at best, and it would have been bad enough if they had just fought us, but to just go behind us and attack the women and children filled us with pain and rage.

I talk of fighting and battles, but in reality, I mostly just remember walking. As always, we walked from one conflict to another. We carried very little: our clothes and guns, while the villages, as always, supplied the rest. But we were always walking. It was at this time that my brother, Mohammed, sent for me. He knew that I was fighting in the Peshmerga as we had been at Siri Rash together, but we had been separated once again. In fact, it was a Peshmerga protocol not to allow siblings to fight together. This was because of the fear of losing two members of the same family in a failed operation. The pain and suffering to the family of losing two or more sons would be tremendous. However, my brother was never one to follow the rules. So during one of our conflicts, my older brother asked me to join his team, and I asked my superiors if I could join him. They agreed, so I excitedly packed up and started walking again.

I moved from the Koya District, which was near the border of Iran, to the Hawler District, some distance away toward the interior. I met up with him and fell right in line behind my older brother, who was still as big, wild, ambitious, and excitable as he ever had seemed in my childhood. Then in a short couple of months, there was another order to move to the Khoshnawti area to fight again. Reports were coming in that the Iraqi Army was attacking there. This time, we went together. Interestingly enough, though, I did not necessarily travel with my brother. He was simply my older brother. He didn't coddle me or make me walk with him. In fact, I usually walked with men closer to my own age. We didn't talk on the road, nor did he give me sage advice. I have thought about why he wanted me with him, and I believe it was simply that I was his little brother, and he felt he could protect me and be responsible for me.

After we arrived in Khoshnawti, we spent some time getting ready for the fight. As I stated before, we were not great strategists. In fact, we often resorted to tactics used from previous conflicts and even the world wars. When we arrived, trucks of equipment were there, and we were ordered to go to the mountains to start digging ditches. We had to hike up to the top of a hill, which was about a two-and-a-half-hour march. This position would give us a vantage point by which we could attack the soldiers marching below. We took pickaxes and shovels to dig ditches in the dirt for cover for when we were attacked. Each ditch was about two to three feet deep, just enough to get your body in and enough to conceal you from attacks or small arms. They were about six feet long, so only about two to three men could fit in each ditch. I dug with my brother. Even though he was older than me and could have bossed me around, he worked just like the rest of the men. He seemed to jump into whatever was happening with such zeal.

Our ditches were also supposed to give us an edge to ambush our enemies. We planned to hide out on the hill and wait for the advancing units to come to us. Then we would pop up and take them all out. It was an ambitious plan at best. We knew we would be fighting tanks, missile and grenade launchers, and heavily armed foot soldiers, while we only had ourselves and our AK-47s.

After our preparations were complete, we waited. There is nothing like waiting for an attack. It is so filled with mixed emotions. On the one side, you are filled with fear and apprehension. Will this be the day I die? On the other side, you are filled with excitement and anger at an enemy who is so inhumane that they can kill innocent women and children. These emotions are enough to drive you into battle, but when you are waiting in a ditch, these emotions almost destroy your mind. The waiting and watching and watching and waiting with little communication is maddening. You have long stretches of utter boredom with nothing but your thoughts to keep you company. Like I said, though, I didn't really talk with my brother. He was mostly concerned with my safety, and he would give me small suggestions on how to hold my gun or how to shoot well. The hours stretched on until finally we got word that the army was approaching.

We were near the top of the small mountain where we could furtively peek out and watch the advancing military. It was a small contingent of soldiers, only about four or five tanks and not more than fifty men walking alongside them. With the element of surprise and a little luck, our small group of about twenty men could take them. When the tanks got in range, we attacked. The advance immediately stopped, and the tanks began a hasty retreat. As the tanks retreated, the support soldiers stepped forward and started firing on our positions.

Years later, when I was living in the United States, a friend asked me to come and see a movie with him. He said it was a great movie about World War II. There was a scene in the movie when the two armies were clashing, the men were hiding in ditches, and shelling and machine-gun fire were spattering all around. I couldn't take it. As soon as the scene started, I was back on that hill with my brother. It was so real I wanted to curl into a ball or run screaming from the theater.

The fighting started out with heavy machine-gun fire from the foot soldiers. Soon, however, the tanks were back in position and started firing as well. We were firing back just as fiercely from our small freshly dug ditches. The fighting seemed to intensify minute by minute as our enemy started taking casualties. In the middle of a battle, the fears, excitement, boredom, and musings completely leave. In fact, it is often difficult for me to remember much of what happened. However, I will remember one experience from this battle until the day I die because it almost was the day I died.

The fighting was getting extremely fierce between the constant bullets and occasional missiles or grenades launched by the soldiers. Soon the tanks which had had to retreat would be back in better positions to start firing on our shallow trenches as well. We were firing intermittently back at them between bursts from our small cover when a Russian-made T-10 armor tank took aim at us and fired. It somehow missed us by less than half a meter. We were both blasted back and covered by dirt and debris. We both sat there stunned and looking at each other, too shocked to even move. My brother suddenly smiled at me in the mischievous grin he used whenever he got away with something. The shelling died down, and we became motionless. With any luck, they thought we were all dead. It still hadn't really hit me how close we had both come to dying together. However, it was not lost on our unit leader, Dr. Rasheed. When the attack had died down sufficiently, he came ducking and running over to check on us. He had seen the projectile and, knowing where we were, feared the worst—two brothers in one shot. I can only imagine what was going on in his mind. He slid down next to our cover and looked at both of us. Surprise and relief in his eyes mingled with worry and incredulity. He shouted to find out if we were okay or injured.

Kurdish Peshmerga leader, Dr. Rasheed

My brother actually laughed in his nonchalant manner, shaking it off, and replied, "Yes, we are okay," obviously dismissing the whole incident as a mere accident of no consequence.

Dr. Rasheed didn't feel that this was "no big deal," however. He immediately made a decision and said, "Karzan [my code name], you have to leave back to headquarters right now." I grumbled to myself in discontent and whined, "I want to stay."

He replied in a tone that offered no argument, "It is not fair to have two brothers in the war zone. Not to your family, not to our cause. Morally, it is not right." He went on in a softer tone, "After all, it is against our policy as well."

I felt burning resentment toward our leader for a time. I was being ordered away from this conflict. It felt like I was being forced to run away—like I was abandoning my post, my friends, and my brother. I did not want anyone to think that I was running away from the fighting. I wanted to show my bravery in the most emotional way possible. I wanted to surrender my life to the cause. As a young Kurd, I volunteered to do this, and I absolutely believed in our fight and our cause. Nevertheless, I had to obey his superiority as a unit leader. As a result, just after a few weeks of fighting alongside my brother, I left and separated from my brother and went back to headquarters, which was at least a day of walking once again.

Despite our fighting and our best efforts, the enemy continued to push farther and farther into our territory. They destroyed town after town and left huge trails of ruin and desolation in their wake. I have to admit, in the end, the Anfal campaign was strategically successful. They destroyed and pillaged the whole northern region.

Iraqi Atrocities

While I was in the mountains fighting for Kurdish rights, as a Peshmerga, I used to hear all sorts of news about how Iraqi intelligence officers and their agents treated our people and how strictly they were operating against our youth, in particular. Once in a while, I received news by word of mouth from friends or relatives about my family. For close to a year, however, my family did not have any news about me, nor did I have any news about them. It seemed as if all that had been another life that I only remembered as a kind of dream. Unfortunately, things were still bad for them.

I remember I saw one of my childhood friends from the village. While we were catching up, he told me about another of our friends, Sarwat, who had been detained by the Iraqi security agents and never came back home. Sarwat was my classmate in sixth grade. He was such a nice and calm boy. He never said anything against anyone. In fact, he really didn't even say anything at all until you really pushed him to talk. I learned that he had been detained for being a member of the secret operator of the PUK Peshmerga. Nevertheless, this was not for sure; it was just speculation. The real reason he was detained is due to allegedly trying to develop some pictures of Kurdish Peshmerga. He had taken the film to a studio that developed pictures. I was told he took the film and dropped them off. He was told to come in a few days to pick them up. When he went back, however, intelligence security officers were waiting for him. They detained him, and he was never seen again.

Years later, when I moved back to the city of Erbil, my friend Sabur told me the full story. Apparently, Sabur was asked by Serwat (the boy who was detained) to go to this place to pick up his pictures. Sabur said, "Sure, I will go with you." Sabur did not know anything about what was going to happen next. However, as soon as they walked into the photo shop, they both were arrested. Sabur was detained as well, along with Serwat. They both disappeared for months, and no one knew where they were even being held.

Serwat Shuker, was martyred by the Iraqi regime

After months of torture, he still did not say anything because he was innocent as far as he was concerned and so had nothing to tell. For Serwat, it was the same thing; but in the eyes and mind of the Iraqi regime, if you develop pictures of Peshmerga or carry guns fighting with them, it is the same thing—you are both Peshmerga. There was no difference between fighting in the mountains or saying something against the regime. The punishment and destiny of that individual are the same, in this case, death. Fortunately, after months, Sabur was let go. He related to me, however, how scared he was after his release from prison. It took him months, perhaps years, to recover psychologically and physically. And for Serwat, to this day, no one knows what happened to him and where he is. Everybody knows he has been killed, but how he was killed or where his body was dropped, no one knows. These are questions that will never be answered for his family or friends.

These were the kinds of reports we used to hear all the time while we were in the mountains fighting the Iraqi government. Often when we hear of these cases, we used to say that at least as Peshmerga, we have the freedom to choose something we believe in and fight for it. These youth in the cities were treated horribly, and their lives were in danger all the time. They did not know when or where they might be detained. For us Peshmerga, at least, we could go out and fight. Some of us will die, and some will return and get ready for another fight. However, this kind of death was honorable, and to the Kurds, we were valued for this.

The news I heard seemed to get worse and worse. Then something unbelievable happened. Another friend brought news that the Iraqi government had razed my village to the ground and no one lived there anymore. All the people were forced to leave their homes and move to concentration camps. Those who were fortunate had families in other places to go and live with. My family was lucky because my father actually had a home in the city, though he preferred to live in the village. Now they were glad to have another house in the city, and they all moved there. They also had enough supplies to survive, thanks to my older brother Bakir. He was still working hard to earn money and support the family.

My brother told me years later about the destruction of our village. He recounted how insulting the soldiers were and the way they treated the Kurds as though they were not even human beings. He recalled how, right in front of all the villagers, they took bulldozers and razed the mosque, the house of God, and unfortunately, God did not do anything to them. There were Qur'ans and beautiful art and all the symbols of our faith, but it did not matter to the brutal Iraqi force. They were simply bent on their quest to destroy Kurdistan and to ensure no one could or would try to help the Peshmerga so that they would find no refuge anywhere. However, when we heard these horror stories about how the regime treated our Kurdish people, we were even more inspired to fight against the Iraqi army.

End of My Peshmerga Journey

After I was separated from my brother, I was told that I needed to go back to my previous unit headquarters. My unit was located in the Kashqa area, which was about a day or two away from the Khoshnawati fighting zone. I left with two men to walk back to headquarters. One of them was a much older man. His name was Mam Aziz, but we all called him Uncle Aziz. Uncle Aziz was about ten to fifteen years older than me. He was tall with dark facial features. He always wore the older Kurdish traditional clothing, which often set him apart from other younger volunteers. He was also a heavy smoker, and whenever he laughed, which was often, his green-yellow teeth showed between his dark lips. I would beg God in my mind to make him stop laughing. He was going with me because he had been injured previously. In fact, he had already missed the recent conflict on the hill because he was healing from his wound. The other guy was closer to my age, probably older by only a couple of years. His name was Muhseen. He was sent to the unit headquarters because he was sick. Muhseen had a light facial complexion and short hair. He was much heavier than me, and sometimes, I could feel this effect when he was walking, as he had a hard time keeping up with us. In addition to the weight, he was still healing from an older previous wound he had on his leg. The three of us were really on our own with no guidance whatsoever from the unit leader. We were simply told to return to headquarters, so we shouldered our weapons and clothes bundles and started walking. Uncle Aziz took the lead in our small group. Musheen and I pretty much listened to anything Uncle Aziz said. We followed his ideas in whatever he told us to do. After all, he was the one with the most experience, and he was older than us. He got us safely and quickly back to the headquarters.

It was not long after we arrived at headquarters. It was not like a military base. We actually were just in a small house. The whole valley had small dwellings for various people. We stopped and stayed for a day or two at one of these places when the whole main unit and area headquarters were targeted by the Iraqi military. We knew that we had to leave. Luckily, there was a truck there for whoever needed it, and we surely did at that point. I was still with Uncle Aziz and Musheen when we left the area. Most of the headquarters had already been abandoned when we decided to leave, so we took the truck to see if we could get to one of the closer villages. It seemed as if, in an instant, our mindset had changed completely: we were no longer Peshmerga; we were in survival mode.

After we left the headquarters, we heard from the villagers and others that the Iraqi military was coming en masse. Soon, we could hear helicopters hovering around the region, shooting at everything moving in the area. The area apparently was now considered by the Iraqi government to be forbidden, and anyone living in the region was either assumed to be a Peshmerga rebel or part of the Peshmerga movement. We had called it a Free Zone, but the Iraqi government called it a subversive area. We also had information from the PUK official sources and leaders that the Iraqi government was increasing the Anfal campaign against us and, in particular, against the PUK Free Zones, which were under our control. Initially, we were driving randomly, but then we realized that we might be running for a while, and we were not ready for a long escape. Fortunately, we had decided to scavenge for whatever supplies we could find from our unit headquarters before we left. We now realized that there would be no safe zones or villages anymore, so we drove like mad into the hills to find a place to hide. We knew it would be a long shot to hide for any amount of time from the horde of Iraqis advancing, but the alternative was defeat and sure death, so we needed to try.

We drove without any particular destination, just trying to stay ahead of any military operation. We would usually only stay a short time in one area a day or two at the most. We tried to keep driving to different locations and move around the region a lot. One day, we were parked in a small valley. It was about four or five in the afternoon. We were about to pack up again to move to a different location when we heard helicopters in the distance. We looked up a nearby hill and saw a massive group of military personnel cresting slowly over the top of the hill toward our position. All three of us were looking at the force on the top of the hill who could not help but see the truck and three men staring back at them. As soon as they realized we were there, they started shooting at us with their machine guns, even though we were still about two miles away. It would have been impossible for them to hit us at such a distance, but they were not trying to hit us; they simply wanted us to know they were there and they were coming for us. Since we were so far away, we knew it would be more difficult for them to watch us if we left on foot instead of driving away, so we decided to leave the truck. We slowly moved away from them to get behind the truck. Then we dropped to our bellies in the sparse bushes and grasses and started furtively crawling away from the truck, leaving it where it was for the soldiers to have a standing target. When my two companions finally snuck over the hill we were camped at, we started running. The soldiers would know this region. Even from that distance, we could tell that there were Kurdish jash with them. It would only be a few minutes before they found our truck and started guessing what we had done; we needed to put as much distance as possible between us and them before they realized we were no longer with our truck.

After that, we were on the run again but on foot this time. Following our desperate initial escape, we stopped at a secluded place that we knew would be relatively safe for a moment. We crouched together to figure out what we were going to do next. As usual, Muhseen and I both looked to Uncle Aziz for what to do next. To our surprise, Uncle Aziz told us he was going into hiding by himself. He didn't care what we did as long as we did not follow him. I am not sure if he was trying to protect us since he was still healing or if he felt we were slowing him down and felt he had a better chance on his own. In either case, he picked up his meager supplies and walked away. Muhseen and I, however, decided to stick together for the time being. We knew we were being tracked and that we were now in occupied enemy territory. So we started running again. Hours turned to days, and our mad run turned into a fast walk. The days of walking turned into weeks. We were forced to constantly

140

keep moving, fleeing from one location to another. We hid in abandoned and destroyed villages (which seemed to be all of them). The people had all left or been captured or killed. We hid by day in broken homes and drafty sheds, sneaking in darkness from one place to another. It seemed that the entire organization of Peshmerga had deteriorated into fleeing scraps of detachments. It was a tough time to be a Peshmerga, and certainly, there were very few people we could trust anymore. Everyone wanted to find a safe path for themselves, and now frequently, they sold their own comrades or friends to save themselves.

The government had destroyed almost all the villages, the ground had been ravaged, and the land had been infiltrated by the government. Many Kurds were now willing to sell you out to survive themselves. The Iraqi intelligence and army were everywhere, looking for people like me. Many weak individuals betrayed each other in order to save their own lives. If they could be seen helping the Iraqi soldiers, they felt they might be spared the atrocities that had befallen so many of their neighboring villages. One of the well-known betrayals at the time happened from Salah Sheene, who was, at one time, one of the best Peshmerga fighters against the Iraqi government. He had been highly renowned and respected by all the rebels. To survive, however, he turned informer and started actively hunting Peshmerga and his former allies and friends. He sold his own best friend, Hayni, to the Iraqi intelligence; and after that, Hayni was never seen again.

I remember one night, after my friend and I had started hiding on our own, we came across Salah Sheene when he was still a Peshmerga. He was close to the main Kirkuk-Halwer Highway, driving a nice Toyota pickup truck with more than ten Peshmerga with him. We saw him at one of the poultry factories—a chicken ranch. We just said hi to him and his group. At the time, he was not working for the Iraqi intelligence office, but it must have been just days before he established his connections with the Iraqi intelligence. Later on, when we heard that the brave Salah Sheene official was now working for the Iraqi government, we couldn't believe our ears.

The well-known high-ranking Kurdish Peshmerga officer (Salah Sheene), after surrendering himself to the Iraqi government, was looking for Peshmerga everywhere. He knew the area very well, and I know of one time more than ten Peshmerga were sold to the Iraqi intelligence by him. He and many other rebels betrayed their own people and went to work for the Iraqi intelligence office. This particular officer was infamously ruthless. It became well known that he was actively helping the army to apprehend members of the resistance and hand them over to the security officers. There was only one punishment for such captives, and it was to be killed—even for his best friend. His betrayed comrade was never seen alive again. In fact, no one even knows where his body is to this day.

Dry Water Well

Every once in a while here in the United States, I have been invited to go camping. My friends here seem to really enjoy getting out in the wilderness without plumbing, soft beds, phones, or all the conveniences of a modern kitchen. Don't get me wrong—I love walking in nature, going on day hikes, and enjoying trips to lakes and parks. I don't even mind sitting around a campfire and swapping stories late into the night, watching the stars come out. I just really hate staying the night. I know why I hate camping so much. It's because I feel like most of my life, by American standards, was actually "camping." When I was small in the village of Peerdawood, there was no plumbing or electricity. We used an outhouse, slept on rough mats placed right on the dirt floors, and had no refrigeration. It was even worse when I was in the Peshmerga. However, the time I spent in hiding was totally different. We were no longer a confident, engaged, loyal band of brothers. Now I was alone, scared, and betrayed. The discomforts I had endured for so long that I simply accepted as part of my sacrifice for my people were now accentuated and painful. I spent so many days eating and drinking terrible food and water, and many more just going hungry. My sleeping was rough and frequently interrupted by sounds and sickness. Now that I have a safe, warm home and a comfortable mattress to sleep on, it is inconceivable for me to want to spend the night outside on the ground.

It was a scary time for all Kurdish people and, in particular, for individuals like me. No one was safe; but my family knew, as did I, that I was definitely one of those people in the most danger. I was convinced that I would never make it out of this situation alive. Too many of my friends had been captured, and I knew it was only a matter of time until I would either be killed or detained, which would essentially amount to the same end. My friend and I were still together, hiding during the day and coming out at night like nocturnal rats or bats to scurry from our latest hiding spot to find another hole to fly furtively to another cave to hide in. I remember one particularly uncomfortable spot and one that later came back as a memory years later when Saddam himself was found. We decided to hide in a dry water well near enough to my people that they could help out, but really it was in the middle of nowhere. It was abandoned, so unless someone informed the government, it was not likely they would find us. There were many such wells in the region. So many people had dug looking for underground aquifers. Most of them came up empty, and nobody ever took the time to fill them in.

The wells were about ten meters deep (thirty feet deep). It was damp and cold down there and dark as night. It was only about a meter in diameter, so there was no room to really move around for two people. Like most wells in the region, it was dug at a steep diagonal. There were rudimentary steps to the bottom, but it was very steep. We had to literally crawl down the shaft and then climb out. Fortunately, it was not too deep. There were many stories about people being trapped in wells and dying because they couldn't get out. Often snakes and scorpions would make their homes at the bottom of these wells. I had to kill several scorpions, but fortunately, we never saw any snakes. I had grown up in the area and had killed snakes a lot, but I still didn't want to encounter one at the bottom of a deep well.

When we got out of the well at night and walked around, we had to walk in the dirt, and it would leave tracks, so we were very careful to make sure that we didn't leave any footprints. We even walked backward and brushed the trail out to make our passing disappear. The hiding place was hard for both of us. The food was provided by a friend of my family. Most of the time, our lunch, breakfast, and dinner were only boiled eggs with bread. We would climb out of the well to get the food. It was so painful to come into the night. Even a bright full moon was too bright for our eyes. If we needed to pee or something, we had to use the same location. Whenever one of us needed to defecate, the other respectfully turned around in that cramped space to let the other person get comfortable until he was done. Another hard part was that we had to make sure that after dark, we took our stools out so that the smell would not kill us while we were using the location. Quite often, due to the poor food and lack of movement, the smells emanating from our bodies were tremendous. Releasing gas was shameful and frequent. We became very open with each other and very sorry for the discomfort we added to the situation. We couldn't lie down and stretch out to sleep, so it was very uncomfortable. There was no air circulation in the wells, so we never had enough oxygen. This would make us always tired; and we loved getting out at night, moving our cramped sore bodies, and breathing the fresh air.

Despite the terrible conditions we were in, we were both grateful for this blessing of having a safe place where we knew we wouldn't be found. The abandoned dry water well was shown to us by one of my family's best friends who owned a poultry factory, basically a chicken ranch. His name was Abdulrahman. Abdulrahman, God bless his soul! He was never found out for his bravery, and he only passed away a few years ago in peace. It was because of my older brothers and my parents that he knew about me and agreed to help Muhseer and me. He already knew of one of these holes out in the country and agreed to help us to hide and feed us, even with the knowledge that if he were caught, he and his entire family would be executed. Eventually, when things calmed down a bit more, he even gave me a place to stay with them at their ranch.

Staying at the Ranch

After a month or so of surviving in the empty well, my friend and I decided to split up and seek our fortunes apart to save our own lives and escape from that fetid hole. He left, and it was only years later that I found out he had turned to the Iraqis and become jash as well. After he left, the family friend who had been supplying us with food and information during that time invited me to their farm, which was very close to the main highway to the city of Erbil, where my family lives now. My older brother Bakir had made all the arrangements with Rahman's family to support me during my hiding.

I am still so grateful for their willingness to assist me. Very few people would have done such a risky thing during that time. As I had seen firsthand, it was more likely that people would shun you or even betray you rather than actually help. I could not blame them either. By taking in a Peshmerga, they would endanger their entire family. If the Iraqi intelligence had found that Abdulrahman was assisting me, they all would have been hanged or shot, even their small children. It was the hardest thing anyone could do for someone like me at that time. For this reason, I will always look on him and his family as guardian angels. Abdulrahman told me that I could stay with them until my brother made other arrangements. Kurdistan was becoming a dead zone. The army was stationed everywhere, along with the despised Kurdish jash—the little jackasses. However, I was still young, and I had escaped again. I was beginning to get bold and restless again. It seemed to me that things were not as serious as everyone kept saying. I had faced death so much that I was becoming careless with my life. I did not know what was going to happen to me or if my life was going to be shortened due to the current situation I was experiencing.

Where I was staying, there was another family, which was their relative. They had a young man a few years older than me. His name was Sayfadeen. He had a small motorcycle, and I started to ride with him in the outer country and then to a small town nearby, Qushtepe. We even decided at one point to see the concentration camp which was built for the Barzani families in the 1980s. It was very risky to do that, and had I been caught, it would have put my new friend, my family's friends, my brother, and perhaps my whole family in mortal danger. But for a young man like me, I did not think or care about whatever might happen. Fortunately, we were never discovered, but after the family found out what my friend and I were doing, Abdulrahman talked to me with his family, and then they talked to both of us and demanded that we stop this. He argued that I would be detained by the Iraqi security office and would never be seen again.

My mother was one of those who worried more than anyone was. She came to the ranch and begged me not to do that again. Their pleas and logic worked on our immature brains somehow, and we stopped going to the town. I began to see how serious that could be for both of us. For him, he was not a Peshmerga, but still, he was a military fugitive. If we were detained, for sure, both of us would be treated the same way since the Iraqi government used to call us, in Arabic, Mukhareeb (saboteurs).

At the moment, the Iraqi government had sent rumors that they would accept the surrender of rebel soldiers. However, it was still important that you found someone that you could trust. You needed someone who could negotiate a peaceful surrender to the Iraqi government with the guarantee that you would not be harmed.

My brother was still out looking for someone whom he could pay to do the job. It was very brave of my brother to risk even attempting to secure my safe surrender. Fortunately, after a few months, my brother told me that he had been talking to a friend and that he had found a way to rescue me from the current situation.

When he found this possibility, he decided to come himself to the ranch to tell me. My family knew where I was hiding, but since my benefactor was an old family friend, it did not seem inappropriate to visit the farm. From time to time, however, my sisters or mother used to come over on the pretext of visiting Abdulrahman, but really it was to see me. However, it was not very often because they were afraid they might be watched as they had two sons allegedly fighting for the Kurds. Therefore, they only came every once in a while because they did not want people to know about me or my location.

After a few months, word came from my brother Bakir to get ready. He said that he had found someone to take us to the security—Mukhabarat office. This "friend" had promised me immunity.

My brother swore that he would protect me and nothing would happen to me. He had paid this man some money. He also produced an old AK-47 and told me not to take my current AK-47 to surrender because that one belonged to the Kurdish Revolution PUK. Even in our surrender, we were still loyal to the cause. He had bought me another one to take with me.

One afternoon soon after, my brother Bakir came and picked me up from where I was staying. As soon as we arrived at the main highway, I saw a couple of trucks full of special teams made of armed Iraqi Kurds (jash), as we called them. It was a moment that was hard to forget. I was thinking just a few days or weeks ago, I was fighting these people. Now I am walking toward them and giving myself up to them. I thought of all the betrayals I had heard of and inwardly trembled with fear since I now had to trust my life to them and whatever destiny would give me.

My brother handed them my "gun," and then I jumped in the back of the truck and sat between the Kurdish jash. My brother followed behind in his truck. First, they went through a checkpoint to enter the city of Erbil. With each jolt, turn, and checkpoint, I was going deeper and deeper into enemy territory. I know what it must feel like for a fly to be dragged deep into a spider's web. I was feeling anxious and scared, regardless of what my brother had promised me. He was now no better off or in any better position than I was. Soon enough, the truck pulled into a parking lot outside a local inn which was being used by Abdulah and Abdul Khaliq special Kurdish officers working with Iraqi intelligence. I got off and was told to go into one of the inn's rooms. I waited a couple of minutes with my brother in apprehension. He, on the other, had worn his confident mask of certainty. He was neither worried nor shaken. We were waiting for his contact, the person whom we were supposed to trust. In a few minutes, he showed up and said hi. He was a slick man—well-groomed and smiling from ear to ear. He spoke confidently and smoothly. His voice and manners exuded trust and confidence. We shook hands, and while shaking, he looked at me and, with a smile, noted, "You look like a disco." This was a common term at that day to describe a person with a modern urbanized city style. "You are one good-looking Peshmerga." He almost winked with his compliment. He introduced himself as Abdullah, and I could tell he was trying to put me at ease, and it was working. We soon got down to business, and he gave us the details of what he was going to do. My task was to come to his headquarters every day that week. At some point, he would be able to take me to the Security Intelligence Office. I also needed to take twelve pictures and bring them with me the next day.

Instead of returning to the ranch, now that I had surrendered, I was free to go back to my family. I had been with them for over two years. I had only seen them intermittently when I was in hiding or when they had come to the military headquarters to visit me. It was so good to be with them with hot meals and people who loved me.

I faithfully went to the daily meetings with Abdullah and had gone there for a few days; and still, I was not taken anywhere. I was amazed to see some of my Peshmerga friends there as well. One of them was a well-known commander, Shero. One day, he looked at me and said, "Do not worry. You see, I was a PUK commander. I am here as well." He had more than a dozen Peshmerga with him who surrendered to the same office my brother used. We had put all our eggs in one basket. We really did not have a choice. We simply had to trust this man.

Shero never came back to that office, and I assumed, when he had surrendered and was fully investigated, all had gone well. It was not until years later, in the uprising of 1991, that we found out that Shero and his group had all been buried alive. The Iraqi security officers had had a large hole dug in one of the well-known cemeteries close to the city with a bulldozer, and the men were unceremoniously bound and tossed in. The officers buried more than 120 individuals in the same pit while the men were still alive. Of course, this was not known until years later when the PUK found and told all our people.

Finally, after a couple of weeks of going to this man's headquarters, I was taken to the Mukhabarat office with Abdullah. This was the official place for me to surrender. He warned me not to talk at all. He was going to speak in his perfect Arabic with the officer in my defense. I stayed there for fifteen minutes; the officer asked me what I was doing on the mountain. This was a saying that they had for

Peshmerga. They simply called us people in the mountains. Abdullah deflected the questions and told the officer that I was a simple baker. He asked me many other questions: had I shot any Iraqi soldiers? I answered dispassionately with a simple no. He asked me where the Peshmerga were located, where I had fought the army, how many people I was with, etc. I answered negatively to all his questions and feigned ignorance of everything. After the lengthy interrogation, he told me to come back in a couple of weeks and bring twelve more pictures.

After this encounter, however, I had had enough of trusting the Iraqi military and the smooth-talking Abdullah. I never went back. However, if I had gone back for the second time, there was probably very little chance I would have ever been seen again. My brother said they had done the same thing to Shero and the rest of the Peshmerga who surrendered themselves. At the time, they had just disappeared, and that in itself was suspicious for a group of fighters with apparent immunity. My brother, when he found out I didn't go back, breathed, "You could have been one of them as well. However, you are lucky that you had someone [referring to himself] who told Abdullah 'this boy must be protected at all costs.' You will be responsible if anything happens to him." I realized that Abdullah had, in fact, protected me as far as that goes. I was safe, but not my colleagues and comrades. Most of them were killed, and their bodies have not been seen again to this day.

As I write this memoir, I want to express my gratitude to Nawzad, who was my brother's friend who saved me. He was the one who threatened Abdullah. If it were not for him, I would have been dead like the rest of my Peshmerga friends. And I must say that I have not been loyal in that respect to thank him in person. I could have done that when I visited Kurdistan many times. But I thank him here. With all my heart, thank you, Nawzad, for my life and now the future of my family as well.

Chapter 5

Civilian Life after Defiance

Prison and Fugitive

Imagine joining a large corporation that you have always wanted to be part of. You work as hard as possible, doing any small job they require just because you love this company and want them to succeed. Then one day, you show up to work, but the doors are locked; and there is a sign on the front door that says the company is bankrupt and you no longer have a job. That was essentially the situation I suddenly faced but much worse.

After many years of fighting, I lost so many friends and family members, and so many villages and towns were destroyed as of result of our fighting. I was very discouraged and saw myself as a failure. I had worked so hard and sacrificed so much, and all the efforts I had put in had come to nothing. I could not reap the benefits from years of fighting for my people. It was not easy to look at the other people in Kurdistan. I remembered the words of so many of the villages and even my own family when they said that becoming a Peshmerga would not change anything. After surrendering, I hated to see that they were right. I questioned whether I should have joined the Peshmerga at all. "What have I done?" I asked myself over and over. Did it make any difference? I was not sure, but the fighting for sure never ended, and our people were still oppressed. We as a people would continue, though. I knew this, even in my most bitter and depressing moments. We had survived and carried on through centuries of oppression and dismissal. We would continue to resist no matter what happened or how strong the opposing government was.

Instead of returning for the investigation then, I simply returned to my family life in Erbil. I began being a civilian again and did not mention my life as a rebel Peshmerga freedom fighter. The conflict was over as far as I was concerned at that point. We had lost, and I was lucky to have survived when so many of my companions had not.

However, after returning to Erbil and becoming a civilian again and supposedly leaving the life of a Peshmerga behind, I began to worry about my safety and future. I was still in limbo. Legally, I was wanted and could be arrested at any time. This situation also put my family at risk. In addition, I had been fighting for so long that I found it difficult to simply sleep in a bed and go to work every day. Soon, I found my way back to talking with Abdullah. I remember many walks going back and forth to the Erbil Intelligence Office with Abdullah. It was natural then that I was spending most of my time at Abdullah's Inn. One day, Abdullah came to the inn and said, "Let me talk to you." He took me to his room and sat me down. He turned to me and, with a straight face with no hint of humor or sarcasm, said, "Right now, I believe for you it is the best thing to enlist in the Iraqi army." My mind started spinning with doubt and thoughts of betrayal. I knew that what he was saying made sense logically for my safety, but my mind and heart were suddenly thrust into momentous upheaval. Seeing the apprehension on my face, he continued, "Things are not getting better for your people, and considering the current situation and political climate, that is my suggestion." He looked at me for a time, perhaps waiting for a reply. When I just continued to stare, he went on, "By doing that, number one, you do not need to visit the Erbil intelligence office anymore. Also, you will disappear from your neighbors and people you know. Thus, there can be no one to turn you in or report on your behavior." He looked me right in the eye with his final argument that rang the final blow and pierced me to my core: "People will no longer see you as a former Peshmerga."

At that moment, I knew it was over. All my years of fighting seemed to swim before my eyes. I had seen such atrocities. Our people had fought, died, run, died, pleaded in dust and mud, surrendered, and died. I remembered the two brothers who were Peshmerga who had run hidden in my small village on my first day of school. How they had resisted and died as martyrs. How we idolized them as children. How much I wanted to join them. How I had joined them and suffered willingly. Now it seemed it was all for naught. The people we had tried to free no longer wanted the Peshmerga. We were not heroes; we were fugitives. "The people will no longer see you as a former Peshmerga." I thought once more of the woman who called me back as a starving boy to give me some bread and yogurt soda. Was I betraying them all now? Had I failed? Was I just to survive? I was too young for these decisions. I wanted to live. I wanted to live.

I ultimately listened to Abdullah's advice. I did not go back to the office of the Iraqi Intelligence Department in Erbil. Even though, in the back of my mind, I was scared that he was giving up on me and selling me to the Iraqi government, I had to listen to him and do as he suggested. There was no one else to trust or turn to. There was no other option. It was not an easy decision. I felt like I was betraying my family, my people, my honor, and myself. I had a talk with my brother Bakir, who was serving in the Iraqi army at the time, and he simply said that we had to do what Abdullah said. Hearing this from my own family helped ease one of my fears. I was scared due to my older brother Mohammed, who was still a Peshmerga. If the government knew I still had a brother in the rebel Peshmerga, I could be in deep trouble. My brother was still hiding or fighting out there with the remaining pockets of Peshmerga. The last we had heard was he was fighting out on the Qandeel Mountain, which was the last holdout for the PUK fighters. He was part of the last pocket of resistance on the Iraq-Iran border until they were eventually pushed all the way to Iran. The Iraq-Iran War was still going on, but there was a rumor that it was going to stop very soon. Mohammed eventually did surrender when Saddam announced a general amnesty to those Kurdish youths who were fugitives or Peshmerga if they would serve in the

Iraqi Army. Mohammed did not come home right away, but almost a year later, he also came back to surrender in Erbil.

It was during this time that Abdullah suggested I enlist. So after the Iraqi regime announced a general amnesty for the army fugitives and those who served as Peshmerga, and due to the urgings of my family and Abdullah, I went to the army recruiting base to register. The process went seamlessly and so quickly that in just over a month, I was assigned to the Erbil army base. I stayed there for only another month or so, and then I was transferred to the Basra front zone. The zone was called Jazeera Al Majnoon (Crazy Island), which was the frontline during the Iraq-Iran War. On August 20, 1988, the Iraq-Iran War stopped.

I never saw Abdullah or his brother Abdulkhaliq again. They had a sad fate for their corruption and betrayal. I was not there, but after the uprisings in 1991, years later, both of them were dragged into the streets by the PUK and shot in front of the people for the stealing that they had done against the Kurdish people in Erbil. I was one of only a few lucky youths who had survived their "advice" and only because of the great risk and payment my brother Bakir had given and the bravery and force of Nawzad, who made sure that the two brothers had not sold me to the Iraqi forces to be killed.

I stayed there for a year or so, during which time Saddam made his fateful international mistake. Up until now, Iraq had been in domestic disputes and border skirmishes, which had largely been ignored by the international community. However, when Iraq invaded Kuwait in August of 1990, the whole world took notice. In fear of retaliation, many Iraqi soldiers were transferred to the Saudi Arabian border. Sure enough, within a few weeks, my unit was transferred to the opposite side of Iraq from my home as well. Our unit was stationed there for a few more months. There was no activity, and life in the Iraqi military was terrible. Morale and discipline were low due to the forced enlistment of so many youths, along with the continued enrollment of former rebel Peshmerga who had no love or respect for the Iraqi regime, only distrust. There were food shortages as well, which caused constant discomfort. I can still feel the disgusting texture of the hard, dried bread. It was like eating dried mud. As a Peshmerga, I had stoically gone hungry, cold, tired, and sore; but it was for the love of my people. Here, to put it bluntly, few, if any, soldiers actually wanted to fight for Iraq.

I was only there a couple of months before I was given a pass with permission to visit my family back in Erbil. I was supposed to return directly to the border. However, I had had enough of military life. I deserted and never went back to the army. This was perhaps another narrow escape in my life because it was only one or two weeks later that the coalition forces attacked Iraq to expel them from Kuwait. I was AWOL with my family, hundreds of miles away, when the full force of the international military led by the US attacked the forces I had only recently abandoned. I have no idea how many were killed, captured, or what. I only know that our unit was one of the front lines that would have been attacked first.

Military Prison

Now, however, I was a double fugitive. I had fought against the Iraqi regime as a Peshmerga, and then when I had been granted amnesty by joining the military, I had deserted that too. In Iraq, only those who followed the regime's protocols were allowed to have IDs to work or move about the country freely. My brother Burhan had also abandoned the military, so neither of us had IDs, and we knew any exposure might lead to our arrests.

It was the beginning of the year 1991, and I realized that I had been officially branded a fugitive by the Iraqi government. I imme-diately went into hiding again, fearing for my life and the lives of my family. This only lasted for a month or so because I had had enough of hiding to last me a lifetime. I just couldn't do it anymore. I decided to go back home and just lie low. Somehow, however, my intentions just never seem to work out. One day, I was sitting at home, well away from danger and the crowds in the heavily watched downtown, when one of my brother's friends, Ismail, suggested that we should go downtown to see the city and shop or something. I incredulously told him that I was still a fugitive and that I didn't want to be arrested by the Iraqi security services. He smirked and assured me that they were easy to see and that I was being a coward. "If we see them, we will just avoid them," he reasoned.

Somehow, his words convinced my young mind to forget the danger. As I said, I had been cooped up too long. I should never have gone at all. Nevertheless, a few hours later, I found myself striding through the crowded, noisy downtown bazaar, enjoying the smells, sights, and people who filled the streets. We had forgotten our fears of being caught and strolled aimlessly without the caution we had promised to keep. Suddenly, as if out of nowhere, someone was in our faces asking both of us to show our IDs (in Arabic, "Hawyat kum"). We froze. All the fears and self-promises washed over me. I thought of the years of hiding and the care I had once taken to avoid this very thing. Now because of a few moments of risky arrogance, I was caught. We did not have anything with us, and they knew both of us were fugitives (young men should be serving in the military, so those who do not serve in the Iraqi army would not have IDs). As a result, we both were forcibly arrested and immediately taken by military vehicle to the prison. After sitting in silence for a little bit, my friend whispered to me that he had some military blank permission forms and handed me one to fill out. He quickly filled out his while we were driving, and he showed it to them when we stopped. They released him and turned to me. Unfortunately, I had not had enough time to fill out the fake permission form, so I was processed as a criminal and quickly transferred to the military prison at the Erbil Military Base.

The coalition air campaign had already started against the Iraqi government, so while I was in the Iraqi Army prison, we constantly heard the sounds of planes, bombs, and antiaircraft artillery. We were in a prison, so we considered ourselves safe from these attacks. One night, however, the base was bombarded by coalition aircraft. Fortunately for us, they did not hit the building we were in. I was not sure if the coalition forces had information about each of the buildings or if we were just lucky. Either way, we were safe from the bombardment.

That same night at about 2:00 a.m., we were forced into military vehicles and transferred to a place just outside of Erbil. We realized that we were in elementary school! The Iraqi military was using a children's school as a military prison! We stayed there only for one night. From there, we were transferred to another military prison in Kirkuk by bus.

It's funny thinking back on that night how I should have been scared out of my mind: our base was being bombarded by powerful outside forces. I was a prisoner of war and could have died at any moment. We were being transferred in the middle of the night to who knows where, but all I could think about was having to go pee.

The day before the coalition attack, the guards were being very strict. They wouldn't even allow us to use the toilet. I had to pee really badly, but the guard would not let me go. It seemed an eternity of waiting all that day, and then we were bombarded later that night. When I should have been trembling from fear, I was instead squirming uncontrollably, trying to keep the urine in. Afterward, we were taken and transferred to another location. The location was an abandoned school, which was located in BardaRash Village, a few miles west of the army base. That night, we stayed there, and then they transferred us to Kirkuk military bases. Throughout this whole time, I was still not able to use the bathroom. I have never had such a stomach ache in my life. All I could see was yellow. So when we were transferred to Kirkuk, I was not able to breathe because I needed to pee so badly. The minute we got on the bus, my friend knew about my situation, and he offered a solution. He told me to sit on the back of the bus and handed me a blanket. He whispered, "Try to use the lower step of the bus and pee on the blanket." I did exactly what he told me, but you know that moment when you finally can do what you want but it won't come. Well, I just stood there for, it seemed, an eternity. I had worked so hard to keep from losing it that now I couldn't even relieve myself. Fortunately, it finally came, and it seemed like I was standing there for forty-five minutes to pee. While everyone around me was anxiously waiting to die, my only thought the whole time was to not pee my pants.

We stayed in the Kirkuk prison for over a week—waiting. They told us they were preparing us to transfer to the Baghdad military prison and from there to the frontline Kuwaiti-Iraqi border to fight against the coalitions. Secretly, we also knew they might just shoot us once we arrived at the military base and then bury us in one of the huge unmarked mass graves. No one knew what was going to happen to us, but, for sure, we knew our future was unknown, but most likely, it would end in death. If we went to prison, we would eventually die. If we were sent to the front lines, we would probably die. And since it was impossible that they would just let us go that easily, the only other alternative was that they would just kill us.

When we arrived in Kirkuk's prison, I saw an old Kurdish friend who was a tailor—he used to make my traditional Kurdish clothes— Abdul Waheed. Apparently, he was serving as military police on the base. He just said hi fearfully because he didn't want to be affiliated with a military fugitive.

One evening, someone came to the front of our prison door and ordered, "As I read your name, move out toward the bus and get in." They started calling out names, and we filed out apprehensively and then onto the bus. As soon as they were done with the roll call, the whole Greyhound-like bus, filled with over fifty prisoners, started up. It was late afternoon or early evening, at about six or seven, when they started. So it was just after sunset when the bus pulled away from Kirkuk's prison. There were three guards on the bus—one in the front, one in the middle, and the other one at the end of the bus. They all were carrying AK-47s. None of us were chained or hand-cuffed. We all just sat. It would have been too dangerous with three assault rifles pointed at us to try anything stupid or brave. It was the longest night of my life. I still replay it over and over in my mind. The unknown, the fear, the insanity of it all. We had our first stop in Baghdad. It was about 1:00 a.m. I remember glancing up at the sky. I was shocked to see it was full of stars like when I had been a boy in my small village. I realized that there were very few lights on in the city since the air campaign was still continuing over the Baghdad sky, which meant that every once in a while, a missile would fly overhead.

The streaming light of bullets was still flying all over the Baghdadi sky. We could see through the windows of the bus the coalition air forces bombing different locations and the bright fire-tales of the Iraqi's antiaircraft defense, shooting back at the planes. It was like a firework celebration night. I was filled with emotions. On the one side, I was vengefully satisfied that, at last, Saddam had picked a fight he was not big enough to win, while on the other side, I knew I was in mortal danger by both the bombings and being a prisoner. On the ground, you could see Baghdad was under attack and different buildings were burning. It was a scary sight to witness as we were waiting for the guards to tell us what we needed to do next and maybe reveal our next destination.

After half an hour or so, only two of the guards came back and said something to the driver, who then started driving. Obviously, they were leaving the third guard there. One of the remaining guards took his position at the front, and the other took up a position at the back. A few minutes later, we were told that most of our paperwork was dated incorrectly and that those with incorrect papers would have to be taken back to the Kirkuk prison to make the correction. Their excuse seemed weak, and we wondered what was really going on. On the way back to Kirkuk, we stopped at one of the roadside restaurants to use the bathroom, and some of us were allowed to buy food. During the half-hour wait, we seemed to realize there were only two guards with us. One was in the front, who was slouching tiredly, and the other was an entire bus length behind at the rear of the bus. Suddenly, they didn't seem so menacing. I was seated in the second row behind the driver. There was another guy in front of me, an Arab from the south, a Shiite who was detained on the Iraqi-Turkey border. His name was Haithem. Next to me was another prisoner, Asaad, Kurdish; and across from me was Luqman, another Kurd. While we were waiting, our chatting started to stray to the topic of minimal security and escape.

As the bus was getting ready to move, continuing our drive back to Kirkuk, it must have been about 3:00 a.m. As'aad, Luqman, Haithem, and I hatched a hairbrained scheme to try for a hijacking. If we could attack the guard and just get his AK, then hijacking the bus would be simple. For some reason, we entirely forgot about the guard at the back. Out of sight, out of mind. We knew it would be very hard to do such a thing. However, we were determined to do something. If we were being taken back to the military base, it was not to get our papers dated correctly. Most likely, we were going to be shot to death, and even if we were just processed wrong, we were still going to be killed in the war. Either way, our lives were pretty much over.

Our plan really only had two steps. After making sure we passed the checkpoint in Kirkuk, we planned to attack the guard, one of us grabbing his AK-47 and pulling the trigger to make sure the driver would stop the bus, and then we would hijack the bus and tell him to take us where we wanted to go, simple. As we passed the checkpoint and entered Kirkuk City, Haithem and Asaad both jumped on the sleepy guard. I grabbed the AK-47 and shoved it into Luqman. The other guard was in the back and was probably sleeping. Luqman raised the barrel and cocked it loudly in the quiet bus. The bus driver suddenly slammed on the brakes. The other droopy and sleepy passengers all jolted awake and started shouting and yelling. The driver turned to us with fear and anxiety on his face. He started begging us to please not hijack his bus or hurt him. The guard we had jumped was also begging us not to kill him. We assured them that we did not want to hurt them as long as they followed our directions. We obviously wouldn't let them go, so we told them they were going to take the bus to Erbil, my city.

A lot of prisoners were sleeping and did not know what was going on. When the bus slammed to a stop, there was so much confusion that many of the prisoners jumped through the window and ran while others stayed with us. While Loqman, Haithem, and Asaad were talking to the guard and driver, I grabbed all the paperwork for all the prisoners. They were all sealed and had our names on the envelopes. I read each and gave them back. When I opened my paperwork, I quickly read through it to the end. There at the bottom was written my sentence: death by firing squad.

As we prepared to take the bus, we told the driver, who was a common Iraqi civilian, that he was going to take us to Erbil. We informed him that he was not going to stop the bus when we got close to the checkpoints. The driver's face was contorted with fear. He was crying and begged us to just let him go. He was afraid that the military would kill him and his family if he didn't return with the prisoners. We responded, "Look at all these men on the bus. They will all be killed or sent to the front lines, where they will die anyway. You have no choice. You are driving us to safety. If we die, we die together." While we were still in the city of Kirkuk, a couple of prisoners decided to get off the bus. We let them go with their papers. We also discovered here that one of the guards was missing, and we did not know what had happened to him. We found out later that one of these men actually reported our action to the base, and so most, if not all, of the prisoners who left the bus in Kirkuk were rounded up and executed in front of the other prisoners to show what would happen if you tried to escape.

From Kirkuk to Erbil, there were two more checkpoints. We had only to go through these two checkpoints, and we would be okay. It was getting close to 4:00 a.m. As we drove into Erbil, many more men wanted to depart from us and did not want to be part of our action due to fear for their lives.

We were determined, though, to carry the plan through to the end. Loquman decided that he would put on the military uniform from the guard whom we had overpowered. He already had his AK-47 as well. We decided that as we got closer to the checkpoint, we would slow down a little bit but not stop. We told the driver that he needed to accelerate as soon as we were past the checkpoint and move as quickly as possible. In addition, we told all the prisoners that, when we went through the checkpoints, to make sure they were hiding under their seats until we told them it was safe. We knew one thing for sure that would help us and that we hoped was still true that the Iraqi communication channels had been broken since the coalition air campaign started. If they were working again, we were as good as dead.

As planned, we drove through two of the checkpoints that way. We were never stopped or detained. There were not even any shots fired. When making the plan, we were not sure if we were going to make it; however, we knew for sure that it was worth trying. Somehow, our plan worked, and we soon arrived in Erbil. We stopped as soon as we got into the city. Each one left in every direction, and I never saw anyone after that event.

When I walked to our house, it was about 5:30 a.m. I had another prisoner with me from Shaqlawa, a town nearby, who came with me to my house because he had nowhere else to go. As I opened the main gate of our house, I walked up close to the window and quietly tapped the window. I didn't want to make any noise, afraid that my neighbors might hear. My mother moved the blinds, and when she saw me, she immediately ran to open the door. As she opened the door, my brothers, my father, and my sisters followed her. They all started hugging and kissing me as my friend was watching us. I immediately told my brother what we had done and how we got out of prison. My brother Burhan said, "Okay, let us take you outside the city to hide." I left my house immediately. After we gave my friend a ride to where he wanted to be, they took me to a small town, Ujamaa. This was a collection camp for people who had been displaced from the Anfal campaign. He had a small cheap house there where I could hide safely for the time being.

Just a week later, the uprising started. The government security forces were still in Erbil, but I decided to come back to stay with my family. I didn't think anyone would be looking for me when there was an entire uprising to deal with. One day, when I was back at my house going out with some friends, I saw Abdulwaheed. I remembered I had seen him in Kirkuk while I was in prison there. He was a military police officer there with a very low rank. According to him, he paid a high-ranking official to make sure he was not sent to the Kuwait War.

When I saw him while I was enjoying walking around the town, he said, "After what you guys did, in the morning, they sent out teams to search for the fugitives and arrested more than twenty individuals. You should have seen what they did to them. They all were talking about Loquman and Assad being the masterminds of that hijacking. You should hide. If they arrest you again, they will kill you on sight." I told myself, "I am not worried. The government will vanish very soon. The uprising is coming closer and closer to our city."

For me, it was not something new. Throughout my youth and life, I have always been a risktaker. Fear has never stopped me from doing what I felt was right, whether that was leaving everything to become a member of the Peshmerga or hijacking a bus to save others. We knew what would happen if we were not successful. There was no doubt in my mind I would have been shot by the Iraqi secret service member or I would be hanged to death. Either way, we had a better chance to survive if we took this matter into our own hands and did what needed to be done. I was proud of myself and my friends for risking our lives to save over fifty other lives. We all knew our destiny was unclear, and in most outcomes, we were destined to die. Many never had even the chance we had on that bus, and we took it, and I escaped death once again.

Chapter 6

The Uprising of March 1991

Uprising in 1991

After my narrow escape through the bus hijacking, the country was still in turmoil. It was still the beginning of the year 1991, just a few months after Saddam Hussein had attacked and occupied Kuwait in August of 1990. We had watched in awe as the United States and its allies gathered international forces to force Saddam's military out of Kuwait. They called it "Desert Storm," and it was, in fact, a terrible storm. The air bombardment campaign hit every military installation and destroyed communication bases throughout Iraq, which crippled Saddam's military power.

For about two months, military airplanes were flying all over Iraq and further weakening the position of the Iraqi military. Throughout Iraq, no matter where you lived, you could see and hear the bombardment. In my city, Erbil, there was only one major military base with an airport. Compared with other critical military bases, the Erbil military base did not have that many military installations, especially if you compared Erbil to Baghdad or another regime's military intelligence base throughout Iraq. It took only a few weeks for the Iraqi military to be defeated and leave Kuwait as a devastated country, leaving hundreds, maybe thousands, of dead soldiers.

When the Iraqi force was defeated, George Bush unintentionally or intentionally announced that the allied troops were not interested in overthrowing the regime but that the matter was in the hands of the Iraqi people. This felt like a tacit allowance for an uprising against Saddam's regime. Saddam was at his weakest point ever. The oppressed Kurds in the north and Shiite Arabs from the south saw this as their moment to finally overthrow their oppressors and perhaps win their independence. By March, an uprising against the Iraqi government had begun again.

The uprising in Kurdistan moved swiftly. Within days, the Kurds had liberated all three major Kurdish cities in Kurdistan: Erbil, Sulaimani, and Duhok.

I was involved in the liberation of Erbil or, as was said, in our traditional Kurdish Hawler. That morning, at around ten or eleven, I saw a group of people walking on the main road by our house and chanting, "Death to the Ba'ath regime and death to Saddam." Without hesitation, I joined the group and started chanting as well. The people were armed with anything except their anger and frustration. The people I was walking with had no guns or rocks or sticks. They did not have anything while they were walking toward the main headquarters of the Northern Intelligent Iraqi office. From outside the group, it would have seemed more like a peaceful march or protest, but the intent of the people and myself was to rid ourselves of the rule from Baghdad.

The office was about a mile away from our house where I had joined. As we got closer to the headquarters, I began to hear gunshots. We could hear the rattle of the automatic weapons being trained on the unarmed population. Bullets were flying around us in complete chaos. I turned around to start to find a place to take cover. I saw, at my right shoulder, my younger brother Salah. He was only thirteen years old at the time. I shouted at him angrily, "What are you doing here? When did you get here?" His eyes were bulging, and his face had gone white. He was a frightened animal with no idea what to do. I was now twice as scared. I was unarmed and completely vulnerable with no place to hide, and now my younger brother was right in the middle of it with me. I grabbed his arm and tried to cover him with my body while running to find refuge from the shooting. The group itself was very small. We were only about a group of fifty to sixty people walking in our direction. Many other groups were marching toward the center. We were disorganized and scared now, but so were the soldiers. While running for cover, I noticed that, in fact, a couple of the citizens had guns. I saw a couple of people hit by bullets, and one of them died right away. Another was wounded and was pulled to cover by a couple of protesters. There was an apartment complex near us, so I shoved my brother ahead of me and into the complex to hide. We sat there for what seemed like forever. It was about an hour or two in reality, but the fighting was only intensifying. Just before sunset, we heard a change in tone from outside. There were shouts of encouragement to come out and join the celebration: the headquarters had been cleared by the Peshmerga. When we arrived at the building, we saw so many dead bodies lying on the ground outside the burning offices. They were all mukhabarat—intelligence officers who were killed or shot by the Peshmerga. I did not see any Peshmerga who were killed or martyred, if there were any, they removed the bodies before we arrived. The military installations in Erbil were quickly ransacked, and any guns and ammunition were quickly snatched up. I got an AK-47 and was back in the Peshmerga.

On the evening of Nowruz, which is the Kurdish New Year on March 21, the Peshmerga were called to Kirkuk. This city had always been a point of contention between the Kurds and the Iraqi regime. Even though Kirkuk has always been seen as a city belonging to Kurdistan, it has a very diverse population. The Peshmerga liberated most of the city of Kirkuk and pushed the Iraqi military away from the military base as well.

The biggest fight between the Peshmerga and the Iraqi military was initiated in the city of Kirkuk. It left many dead on both sides. As a Kurd and returning as a Peshmerga, I participated in the uprising. As I remember, Kosrat Ali was organizing the fighting from Erbil's side. As we got closer to the city, we started encountering small pockets of resistance on the Erbil-Kirkuk Road. The biggest obstacle was a large tank on the top of the hill on the right side of the highway. It was firing seemingly randomly at whatever was coming up the road. There were so many volunteered Peshmerga in front of us, an hour or so later swarmed the tank and took it out. It was probably just a diversion to give other soldiers enough time to retreat back into safe places in the city, in particular to the military base named Khalid.

The defense by the military was not well coordinated; nevertheless, it still took a few hours for us to enter the city since we were not organized either. As we entered the city, people were welcoming us and giving us water and food. They could smell freedom just as we could. Our goal was to enter the military base called Khalid. As we were fighting the Iraqi soldiers, I saw men dressed like Kurds fighting on the side of Saddam. One of my friends told me that these people were "Mujahedeen Khalq." They were part of an Iranian rebel militia group that was resisting the regime in Iran and so supported Saddam. As such, these Iranian Kurds were fighting against us alongside the Iraqi soldiers.

After another hour or so, all the Iraqi military were killed. We entered the military base through the main gate. As the Peshmerga continued their fighting, civilians started pouring into the base, and they started looting and taking whatever they found that might be valuable. I entered the Khalid military base, got into a car, and left the base. I wanted to see if I could find my brother's truck.

My older brother Bakir had been called back to serve in the Iraqi military months before the uprising. He was serving in the Jalawla region during Iraq-occupied Kuwait. When the allied forces pushed the Iraqi army back from Kuwait, my brother was still serving in Jalwala. Just weeks before, he had managed to get permission to come home. However, traveling to Erbil, in Kirkuk, Iraqi security detained him, and they took his car as well. They sent him to join another group of the military. He had been forced to leave his small truck behind in Kirkuk. The next day, he ran away from the military anyway and came back home to Erbil but was unable to return to Kirkuk to retrieve his truck.

Since I had left Erbil to join in the operation in Kirkuk and I knew my brother's truck was left in Kirkuk, I decided, in the confusion and apparent victory, it would be an ideal time to get the truck back if it was still there. He told me he had parked his truck on the main highway between Kirkuk and Tikrit. Therefore, the minute I found a car at the military base, I drove there to look for my brother's truck. Luckily, I found it and waited for my brother to come to take it back to Erbil. It was a great sense of relief when we discovered that the truck had not been stolen or ransacked. For my brother and our entire family, it was a source of income to provide food for all of us.

Since I did not have any obligations, and I was not part of any particular groups or belonged to any organized Peshmerga group, I started driving back to Erbil on the evening of March 21, 1991. People had started celebratory bonfires all over to celebrate Nowruz for the first time freely, and it was a day I will never forget. For hundreds of years, Nowruz, our traditional New Year's celebration, had been celebrated with huge pyres in the middle of the towns or the tops of the mountains. The people would sing, eat, and dance around them all night. Now they were celebrating it as independent Kurds with a very bright hope of actual autonomy over their own lands. When I got home, my father was so happy about what I did; he spoke about my action within the family and the neighborhood. I could see the sense of pride shining on his face when he spoke about me.

This jubilation and independence were very short-lived, however. Less than two weeks later, Peshmerga forces were not able to hold Kirkuk. The Iraqi military decided to crush the Peshmerga forces. The considerable forces that the Peshmerga had managed to gather in the short amount of time in Kirkuk were, nevertheless, incomparable to what the Iraqi Army brought to fight against them. Our forces were courageous and fought bravely against overwhelming odds, but the Iraqis led a ruthless military campaign. Hundreds and thousands were left dead in the fighting on both sides. In the end, the Peshmerga could not hold on to the city, and the PUK lost many good Peshmerga, including a few high-ranking commanders. The Kurds had known it would not be easy to protect and retain Kirkuk unless the US had intervened in bombarding the Iraqi military by air. They were hopeful at first due to the animosity between the US and Iraq, but the support, of course, did not happen. Therefore, with the use of helicopters and tanks, the Iraqi military was able to retake control of the city of Kirkuk in less than two weeks. Then the Iraqi military moved forward to my city, Erbil.

Just a few days later, the Iraqi army had moved into position outside the city of Erbil in order to reestablish its dominance there as well. I remember that morning very well; I was in the Peshmerga headquarters in Erbil, and my former Peshmerga leader, Mamosta Bakir, asked me to drive him to the bank of the eastern part of Erbil. When we arrived near the edge of the city, we saw Iraqi military helicopters flying above the outskirts of that side while Iraqi tanks were trying to encircle the city to block the north-side highway. It seemed clear that the object of their maneuvers was not to let the Peshmerga or civilians get out of the city alive. As soon as we saw the Iraqi helicopter and tanks, we sped back to headquarters. Mamosta Bakir was determined to let the commander Kak Kosrat know where the Iraqi military was and what they were doing. Kak Kosrat had been put in as head of operations in Erbil for the PUK. We went back to the headquarters: a place called Markaz Al Shabab,' translated as "Youth Center."

After a few minutes, the decision was made to abandon the city on the west side because the south and east would be completely controlled by the Iraqi Army in a matter of hours. I remember how as word spread to vacate the city, thousands of people took to the roads. Then as we were fleeing through the village called Baharke, Iraqi helicopters swooped overhead like giant vultures and started attacking and firing on defenseless civilians. Women, children, old men, and shopkeepers were all considered enemies of the state now. The Hawler-Salahadeen Highway was becoming a highway of death, with the wounded and dying crying out among the carnage of death that surrounded them. I did not join the rest of the Peshmerga but left my unit to go by myself at this point. I wanted to find my family to make sure they were safe. I was driving an old Volkswagen. In Kurdistan, they used to call it Brazilee, a small four-door sedan. The road was jammed bumper to bumper until you passed the Saqlwa area. It was nearly impossible to get back into the city because pretty much everyone (over a million people) had left or was trying to leave the city and both sides of traffic were now moving out. I was one of the only people trying to drive back in!

It was impossible to have regular traffic. All rules and order were lost in fear and confusion. Many people were leaving to try to get to the Iranian border. There were people traveling however they could. Those with their vehicles were stuck in traffic honking or trying to drive around or through cross-country. Those without vehicles were walking or riding animals if they happened to have them. You could see trucks, trailers, and small pickup trucks full of people and moving. The scene looked like a doomsday film. It was impossible to comprehend what directions people were heading. They just wanted to leave the city to protect their families. The military did not chase the people but just let them leave. I supposed their taste for blood had been somewhat satiated on the highways. The people on the road, however, were now refugees with no home and no hope of rescue. They had to make it to one of the bordering countries and rely on the mercies of those governments to survive. The trek would take weeks through rough terrain and high mountains. There had not been time to get food or supplies, and it was already late in the season.

As people were leaving toward the mountains and the Iranian-Turkish borders, looking for a safe place where Saddam's army could not reach them, the cold weather set in. The fear and discomfort of terrible traffic and endless walking soon became treacherous the higher they got. Light drizzle in the valley turned to flakes and then snowstorms in the mountains. Those walking or who ran out of gas and were stranded were not prepared for wintery weather. As a result, many people succumbed to the freezing cold right on the road. The most vulnerable were young children, the elderly, and people with chronic diseases and ailments. Weakened as they were from the long march, no food, and the bitter cold, they simply collapsed on the muddy sides of the highway and died. So many grief-stricken families were forced to quickly bury their loved ones on the side of the road with nothing to mark their graves. With such a mass exodus of people, the lack of sanitation caused diseases to run rampant. Necessary sanitation was not available for anyone. It was amazing to see how people used the open fields, small creeks, and banks of rivers as toilets. This tragic scene burned in our eyes, such a pitiful heart-wrenching pain. After all the years of suffering and all our struggles, when we had seemed so close to freedom and autonomy, we found ourselves alone again. For weeks, there was no help from the international community. Finally, the US military started dropping food from the air to these people in the mountains to help.

I couldn't find my family in Erbil, so I escaped with the rest of the people. I continued to look for them in the crowds and among the cars as I drove toward the Iranian border. Finally, I found them in a small town called Soran, close to Iran. I spotted the family truck first, giving thanks that I had gone back to get it those months before. When I saw that truck, I stopped my car and ran over to them. When my mother saw me first, she grabbed me with relief and started kissing and hugging me with tears coming out of her eyes. "Thank God," she said, "you are safe." She did not let me go for what seemed like several minutes. My father smiled and said, "Here you go. You were crying and saying, 'I don't think I will ever see Kamal again.' Now you can feed him, you can hug him, and you can kiss him!" It was such a relief to know they were all safe.

From there, we moved to the Iranian border with my family. It took us another day or two to get to the checkpoint of the Iranian military. We arrived in Peeranshahr, and it looked like the end of the world. It was only a small town, but with the huge influx of refugees, people were moving like little ants all over it. I would never have imagined that such a small town could hold so many people. Families with their children filled the town. Whatever extra rooms there had been were filled. There were makeshift shelters everywhere, and there were some who were just sleeping on the street. Many of them had made the mosque into a temporary place to stay. Some families just stayed in their cars and used blankets to stay warm.

When we arrived at Peeranshar, an older man approached my dad and invited him and our family to his home. I was once again amazed at the benevolent generous side of humanity. It was in complete opposition to the brutality of the soldiers. I was amazed and humbled to see how good this family was to us. They fed us, gave us places to sleep, and sheltered us for weeks. My father was so appreciative of the hospitality of this family. Day and night, he called for blessings down from heaven on them. Even after we left Iran, he continued to praise them and pray for their health and safety. Besides him, we all greatly appreciated what they did for us and how they made room in their small house for our big family. It is impossible to understand that kind of human kindness unless you go through such trials and live in such situations. As long as I am alive, I will always be grateful for what they did for us. I will never forget the face of the head of the family, a tall elderly face with kind eyes. My father always called him Mam Sayed. "Mam" means "uncle," and "sayed" is an honorary term, so he called him "Honored Uncle," as though he was family. Of course, Mam Sayed and his family are all Kurdish from Kurdistan of Iran. We all spoke Kurdish with a little of a regional dialect difference, but with no difficulty understanding each other.

After many weeks, the UN, with the support of the United States, finally decided to intervene on behalf of the Kurdish people. They imposed a no-fly zone over Kurdistan, Iraq, against the Iraqi government to ensure that the people could safely return to their devastated homes. After many lives had been lost and so much destruction had been perpetrated against our people, we were encouraged to move back to our homes. We bid fond farewells to our benefactors in Iran and packed our small truck and drove back across the border into Iraq toward the town of Soran.

Chapter 7

Refugee Camp in Turkey

There, my family left me, and they went back to Erbil. I decided not to return to Erbil for my own safety. I told them since I had been part of the uprising that I didn't trust the government to be able to safely go back to the city. I stayed behind with my cousin Neehmat at Fryed Rawanduzi's house. Fryed Rawanduzi had spent his whole life as a PUK Peshmerga. Mamosta Osman, another very well-known high-ranking PUK member, was also staying with them in that city. Both of them have spent most of their lives being a PUK Peshmerga, and both of them were considered high-ranking PUK members. I am not sure what they were waiting for in Rawanduz, but they could not find a better place for sure to relax and regroup with the PUK commanders. As I spent a few days there with them, I was thinking about how wonderful it would be if I could leave this country. One day, I went to Soran to buy food with my cousin Neehmat, and I overheard someone talking about people going to Turkey. They said, "There is a UN refugee camp in Shamdeenan, and many Kurdish refugees are going there." This felt like the answer to my yearnings. I would leave this war-torn country. As soon as I got back to our place, I told my friends I was leaving. They asked me where I was going. I pulled my gun out and my pair of binoculars that they had supplied me with and placed them on the table. "Here are my gun and my binoculars. I am going to Turkey." They just stared at me, so I continued, "I heard there is a refugee camp, so I am going there, and I do not want to look back to Iraq. I am leaving for good."

I did not have any money, but I just wanted to get out of Iraq. I was young, adventurous, and a bit reckless. I did not consider what was going to happen to me or what journey I had to take to get out of the country that had given me nothing but suffering and difficulty.

I went back to Soran, and there was an old Land Rover taxi parked by the main road and its driver with gray hair calling, "Going to Sheladeze-Sherwan and need two more people to leave." Sheladeze is a small village on the Turkey-Iraq border. I got in and paid in advance, about one Iraqi dinar. On the way, I was talking to two other individuals who were coming from Sulaimania, and they told me they are heading to Turkey as well. We told the driver about our intended destination, so he told us he would let us know when we would need to get off. I'm not sure how long it took us, but after we left Soran, the driver stopped somewhere and said, "Here you go, guys." He let us out and pointed toward a nearby mountain. He explained that that was the place we could go to cross the border. We got out of the taxi. There were four of us. Three Kurdish and one Iranian Pasdaran who did not speak Kurdish, only Farsi. We did not talk that much, but we all knew where we wanted to go. We started walking up to the mountain. It was rigid, but we climbed up to the very top. It was late in the afternoon when we finally reached the top of the mountain. I remember seeing a huge rock with "Turkey-Iraq Border" written on it. There were four of us, and we shared a brief sigh of relief and anticipation between us. We had made it to our new country. Who knew what life awaited us here?

The odd thing was, even though we knew where we eventually wanted to be, none of us knew where it was or how to get to the refugee camp. After we entered Turkey, we walked for another half an hour or so until we arrived at this small village. I am sure someone told us the name of the village, but for sure, I do not remember it. As we entered the village, we went to one of the houses, and they gave us some food. I will never forget what they fed us. It was macaroni. I had never had macaroni in my whole life. This was my first time ever eating macaroni. I hated the taste as there was nothing on it, it was just very dry, and I had a hard time chewing it. I still ate it, though, since I had no choice—I was starving. I needed to eat something to get some energy so I could continue traveling.

One thing we were told by our host was to make sure we were not seen by the Turkish military observers. He warned that if they saw us, they would detain us, or they might just kill us. He also informed us that we could take the main road and it would take us to Shamdeenan, where the refugee camp was located. He added, "But don't be seen!" We were advised to avoid military checkpoints, which were usually on the top of the mountain from one destination to another. He told us to try to move around them. Meaning, climb up to the mountain, and go around them at night so they cannot see you. We did exactly what we were told for two days and nights. During the day, we hid and waited until it got dark and then moved around the mountain points from one place to another.

The journey was hard, and we were very tired. I will never forget the second day in the morning we were climbing up the mountain for our final destination. As we reached the top of the mountain, we climbed to avoid the military checkpoint. We came out over a steep mountain slide that was overlooking the Shamdeenan town. Looking at the town on the top of the mountain, there was no trail to climb down. We spent a few minutes arguing about how to get down the mountain. Finally, we surmised that the only way we could go down was to just slide slowly on our butts all the way to the bottom of the mountain to get into the town. It was something I cannot forget. I can still feel the pain of the bumps, bruises, and scrapes when I think about it.

As soon as we were down from the mountain, we walked to the market of the town. We saw a couple of Kurdish guys, and we told them we just arrived in town. They took us to the office where we registered our names. The same day, I was given a tent with one of the men I had traveled with. His name was Aso. The UN personnel gave us some food and directions on what we can and cannot do.

After a couple of months of getting used to the camp, the Turkish government decided to transfer all the refugees to the Siloppi town refugee camp, which was located on the Iraq-Turkey border.

The UN and Turkish government brought buses to transfer us to their intended refugee camp. I remember the journey of our driving was about six to seven hours to get there. The minute I saw the camp, I was really disappointed. It was empty and barren and right on the border of Iraq. In fact, from behind the camp fences, you could see the town of Zakho. I thought to myself that the Turkish government just wanted to tempt us with a view of our home to punish us or encourage us to just go back to Iraq. Later on, I found that my assumption was correct. In addition to the barren land and the tempting Iraqi city just beyond the border, the refugee camp itself was a scary sight; the camp was surrounded by concrete walls and military barbed wire. It looked more like a military prison, not a refugee camp.

Dr. Bewar with some friends in a refugee camp in Turkey.

refugee camp—Turkey—Silopi

Silopi is just a few miles away from Zakho City. There is a major border checkpoint from both countries, and it was the main route for trading between Iraq-Turkey.

After moving from the Shamdeenan refugee camp to Silopi in 1991. I lived and stayed there until June 2, 1993. I lived in such hard conditions that no one who hasn't been through a similar experience could imagine. The daily suffering for each of us was beyond understanding. As I reflect, I do not know how I spent over two years under such harsh conditions. The only way I can explain why I stayed when I could have just gone back home is that when an individual makes his or her decision and makes an absolute determination that nothing will deter that decision. As I said before, the Iraqi border was visible from our camp, but I knew if I went home, I would be giving up. The Peshmerga had lost, and my people had been crushed. My own name and opportunities in my country were in jeopardy. If I went back, I would just accept that I would never be anything but a second-class citizen for the rest of my life. I knew I had to make it to a better country, and the only way to do that was to outwait the

176

bureaucracy of the refugee process. No matter how much you suffer as a human being, when it passes, it becomes history.

I went through food shortages, water shortages, bitter cold in the winter, and sweltering heat in the summer, all while living in a simple UN tent. However, nothing could shake the foundation of my vision or could discourage my soul from looking toward the future I pictured in my mind. There was nothing that could defeat me. From what I had envisioned, the future of my life was waiting out there. The harsh Turkish treatment and the terrible living conditions could not stop my dream. I could see the horizon coming to me in the near future. I just kept thinking, "I am going to make it, and I will have a new life."

The refugee camp was set on an empty flat piece of earth. It was obviously part of a military zone and was surrounded by a cement wall with barbed wire around it and razor wire spiraling on top of it. We were exactly welcomed as Kurdish refugees in the country of Turkey.

The UN office was also controlled by a Turkish agent named Isam. He spoke Kurdish, but he was not sympathetic to our plight. All the refugees assumed he was an intelligence officer for the Turkish military, because why else would he carry a gun in a refugee camp! Not only was the UN office run by him, we hardly saw any UN officials who were not Turkish or working directly for the Turkish government. The camp was controlled by the Turkish government.

Once in a while, we would see foreigners coming to the camp. However, while they were walking around the camp and talking to the refugees, Isam was always with them. Most people knew not to say anything that would upset the Turkish government or say disparaging comments about the treatment we were getting. We wanted to get out as soon as possible, and keeping the Turks happy was our best chance. We all understood that the Turks saw all Kurds as a security threat, and so they were treating us as a security threat.

They normally wouldn't really help Kurds, but they accepted refugees because they got money to take in refugees. In reality, they were actually trying to get us to give up and go back home. We were surrounded by the military with guards on towers. If we stepped out of the camp, they considered us as a threat, and at best, we would be forced to return to Iraq. There was nothing we could do, so the best practice was to keep quiet and get a pass that would take us out of the camp and Turkey altogether.

My older brother Bakir with my youngest brother Salah.

Summer and Winter in the Refugee Camp

The camp itself was a disaster. Dusty during the summertime and muddy in the winter. The temperature fluctuated tremendously. During the summertime, we just had to manage ourselves the best we could when the temperature reached over a hundred degrees even in the shade of our dilapidated, rusting, old torn-up tents. The camp was divided into three sections. Single men in one section, single women in another, and families in the third. Sometimes, when I reflect, I wonder how people under such harsh conditions along with their families and children survived. I guess we all had one dream, and that dream needed sacrifices beyond other people's understanding to make them real. We were all determined that nothing would stop us from surviving and getting out of the camp.

As unbearable as the summers were, the winters were worse. During the two winters I lived in the camp, it snowed both times. They told us that it was the first two times in forty years. Even when it wasn't snowing, it was always raining. The dusty ground turned to sticky mud. It stuck to our boots and pants. It coated the tents and got on our blankets. That is until it froze.

Whether it was summer or winter, we had to bring water from a pipe on the other side of the camp. We had to fill up whatever water we needed for the day, and then we had to carry it from one place to another or to our own tent, depending on where we needed it. The hardest part was, during the wintertime, to get water in plastic containers and carry them to the tent in the slippery sticky mud. I believe, my least favorite part, though, was taking showers during the wintertime with the cold water. There was only one bathroom and shower area for the whole camp, though it was separated for men and women. Often, I waited for as much as I could to avoid taking showers during the wintertime. I wanted to make sure that I would not get sick by taking a cold shower in the bitter cold. However, sometimes, I was forced to take one because I could smell how horrible I smelled. By then, I just needed to endure the punishment.

Food and Camp

Food is sacred. I have known that respecting food is not an option; one must undertake such a duty as a human being. For example, throwing food, especially bread, is forbidden in the Muslim religion and Kurdish culture. I have always been loud and clear throughout my youth life to avoid wasting food. And my personal life experiences taught me that as well.

When I first migrated to Salt Lake City, Utah, I started working as a dishwasher in a restaurant. I witnessed how they wasted food every night at the end of the shift and tossed it in the garbage.

I believe, in this country, the United States, food is so inexpensive that people take that commodity for grand. I wish there were a systematic approach from school and in the household to teach our new generation how to appreciate food and stop wasting it. Food is something I always remind my son (Ari) and my wife to be mindful of not wasting but instead enjoying what they eat. However, living in a refugee camp in Turkey was a unique experience. The government hated us, and they wanted us to suffer in every way to leave even though the UN was paying for our expenses.

Food was sacred throughout the camp and would cost us dearly. If we had anything valuable, we could use it to barter for "real" food. Local merchants would often come to buy from us. They often brought valuable and more nutritious food to sell to us. I remember, when first arrived at the camp, I had my gold ring with me. I had this ring when I was a Peshmerga. My family bought me that ring because they wanted me to have it for an emergency. After a few months in the camp, I was forced to sell the ring. I sold that ring for almost two hundred dollars. It helped me tremendously for months to buy food and other essential needs. After selling my ring, I was able to eat some meat! I had not had meat since arriving in the camp. It was so amazing to eat some chicken with rice. For months, I was dreaming of good-quality food, in particular meat and rice.

It is difficult to take two years inside a dilapidated refugee camp and quickly summarize it. The days and weeks melded into a confusing mush in my memories. There were few events that broke the monotony of the endless days of waiting. I remember when we first arrived there, the US military distributed a vast amount of canned food for the refugees. Well, it wasn't really varied. In fact, it was just beans. We had large #10 cans of dried beans! The refugees had so many, in fact, that we built walls around our personal tents with them. The walls seemed to give some structure to the camp. They partitioned off the areas, funneled water away from the tents, and (we hoped) discouraged some vermin from entering. Over the months, the supply dwindled, and the walls came down as we slowly ate through our initial rations.

Oh! How I hated those beans. There was an embargo that occurred during the time I was a refugee in Turkey, which meant that no food or supplies were given to us. We got very creative with

the beans: we would fry them, mash them, and boil them. We sometimes even ground them into a kind of flour and tried to bake them
as small flat pancakes. Besides beans, we had a few essentials, as they
called them: a small allowance of sugar, rice, oil, and tea. That was
not much to use to try to be creative. The embargo was because of
Newroz and lasted over a period of a few months. Finally, we started
to get a small bit of other items, such as tomato paste, dried onions,
and some bread. It was not good bread, like my mother made, but it
was bread, nonetheless.

The few times when I would splurge from the money of selling
my ring to get a little meat or some extra spices or a fresh loaf of
bread were the only exceptions to this mundane diet, and it wreaked
havoc on my body. I lost a lot of weight there, and my clothes seemed
to just hang off my limp body. I had very little energy and most days
just sat in the shade of my tent. I was lucky, though, because most of
the inhabitants suffered worse from malnutrition and many got very
sick. It seemed that each wave of catastrophe drove many of the people to abandon their dreams of getting out of Iraq and Turkey. The
embargo caused many to return home. Disease drove others back to
the families. The bland diet and constant lack of nutrition finally
sent others back as well. We would wake up in the morning, and
another tent would be empty or packed up.

The tents themselves were enough to cause many to leave. They
were little more than canvas coverings. They were old, brown, and
falling apart. There was no floor, so we slept on the bare earth, with
only a thin spongy sleeping mat and a worn blanket to lie on. They
leaked when it rained and let in dust when it blew. Bugs—insects,
spiders, beetles, and anything else that wanted to—would fly, crawl,
or tunnel right in to take shelter in the shade. In the winter, it was
little more than a windbreaker and did nothing to keep in any heat.

For heat, we were issued a small propane stove. This served as
our stove and lights as well. We cooked on it, read around it, and
warmed our hands over its small flame. It gave very little light, and at
night, we wanted light to read or write, so my tent mate and I even
got a little creative and made a small pipe out of old aluminum foil
to use as a taper which we attached to the propane stove. By opening

the stove only a small fraction and then allowing only a small opening from the small pipe, we created a very small stream of gas. When we lit the other side, it gave off a small flame which allowed us to see at night. It served our needs but was actually very dangerous. Not only were we lighting the propane tank directly with a makeshift pipe attached, it also made the room smoky, and we got headaches from it and would have to go outside to breathe.

We were constantly dirty. The tents, mats, and blankets were all covered in dust or dried mud. Our clothes were the same clothes that we had arrived in. We would wash them and hang them out to dry and then put them back on. They became just like the tents, old and faded brown. They were tattered and worn and barely held together to cover my body. The summer was bad. Because of the heat and dust, we were sweaty, but we could shower fairly often since we had water and it was cool and felt good. It was in an open recreation area, so there was not a lot of privacy, but I still took advantage of it. The winter, however, was a different story. Because it was so cold and I didn't want to get all wet and possibly catch a cold, I would often go as long as I could without bathing until I couldn't stand my own stench any longer, and then I would get the cold water and bathe. Our lack of hygiene and malnutrition had a devastating effect on our oral health. There were no doctors or dentists, and my teeth were rotting in my mouth. I had cavities and toothaches that made it even more difficult to eat. These I just lived with for the years I was there until I finally made it to a dentist in the United States.

The social structure of the camp was also very depressing. There were somewhere between two thousand to four thousand people who arrived in the camp who hoped to get to the US or Canada, and many of us eventually made it, but many others gave up and returned to Iraq. The camp was divided into families, single women, and single men. As a single male, I was at the bottom of the heap. The families were considered the most important. They got the best resources: tents, water, food, etc. If you had children, you were given priority. Even among the refugees, the families had the most power. After families, single women were also cherished and protected. They would make sure they had what they needed to take care of themselves. The single men were at the bottom. We were considered bums and miscreants. The families avoided talking with us, and they even avoided our part of the camp. The single women would not even look at us. They had good reason to distrust single men as there were many stories and experiences where they had been robbed, abused, and harassed by men who were not attached to a family. The entire time I was there, only a few families were actually kind to me. This was so difficult to me because I had come from such a large and loving family. I was used to small children and older adults around me, giving me counsel, playing games, or even just talking. Now I was automatically judged as a dangerous potential criminal. I remember once I was having a great intellectual conversation with one of the older gentlemen in the camp from one of the families. It was so nice until he found out that I was a single male. His voice became cold and distant, and he quickly found an excuse to cut the conversation short. I never talked with him again.

In addition, there were also economic disparities among the refugees. Many of the refugees came from families that were well-off. They came with more money and received funds from their families. Those who had such means could buy a better position in the camp. Due to both the corruption and the local merchants, if you had money, you could buy better tents, clothes, and food. I was not in that situation. My family had lost so much and could not give me anything. Besides the ring I sold, I had to live on the limited funds provided to every refugee. So, as a poor, single, young Kurdish male, I was at the very bottom of the social structure within a refugee camp in a country that already didn't want us there. Fortunately, due to my friendly nature and honest disposition, I was finally able to make a few friends.

During my time as a Peshmerga, I endured many of the same struggles of extreme heat and bitter cold. I had gone hungry from lack of nutrition and had been pushed and ordered around by both my side and the opposing army. All this was annoying to me, but I had endured it already. The real trial and one that almost seems trivial in explaining it was the pure monotony of the camp. There was absolutely nothing to do but wait. We would sometimes play soccer, if we could get a ball, or we would play simple games that people had brought or that could be played with the dirt and materials we had on hand. I wrote poetry sometimes in a notebook I had brought with me. There were very few books, and we didn't get a lot of news from the outside. After a while, my mind simply stopped trying to stay engaged. I found myself struggling to get up every morning. I would lie lethargically in my tent on my cot, just staring into the canvas. I had lived such an active, curious-filled life that I felt myself almost slipping into madness from inactivity.

Today, I often wonder to myself how I survived that horrible camp. I believe it was because I just kept telling myself that the day would come when I would not be treated this way, the way I had always been treated. I was now a refugee in a country that didn't want me, but before, I had been a second-class citizen in a country that hated my people. Though I hated the life in the camp, I knew that I had to find a place where I could achieve my dreams and live with dignity. And I knew that if I endured, I would not have to live in such a degrading way forever. In those couple of years, so many tragedies happened to my family and me, but I still would not lose my hope of leaving the Middle East, in particular Iraq, and going somewhere to seek a better life. I did not care where I went, I just wanted to leave this region.

My Parents Visit

While I was at the refugee camp, one day, my name was announced through the microphone, which was located in the UN office. When I went to the office, I was told that my mother and father were on the Turkish border, waiting to see me. There was a minivan belonging to the UN office. I got in, and the driver took me to the last point of the border between Iraq-Turkey (Fish Khaboor). As soon as I got out, the driver told one of the police officers, "This guy is here to see his parents, and they are waiting for him." As I walked to the last police checkpoint, I could see that there was military barbed wire dividing the two countries. Then I saw my parents seated on the ground, looking toward me. As I got closer to them, my heart was pounding for two reasons. One, I was happy to see them, and my eyes were all watery. The second reason was I felt bad for them. They had needed to travel all day by car and then stay overnight just to come to see me. I knew the Turkish police and gendarmes were not nice to the Kurdish people at all. At the moment, I felt bad for them. God knew how they were being treated. The good thing was, they were on the other side of the fence, so they did not have to deal with the Turkish authorities that much.

As I approached them, on the other side of the border while I was on the Turkish side, my mother started crying and wanted to touch my hands, so I extended my hands to her. She was sobbing so hard that I had a hard time understanding her. Father said, "Khadij, please thank God he is alive. Be thankful that we could see how he is doing at the refugee camp." We were like prisoners exchanging our conversations for half an hour. A police officer noticed how emotional my mother was and took pity on us. He motioned for me and my parents to move to another area, and there I was able to cross the fence and actually hold my mother and father. My father asked me how I was doing. I said I was well. He asked me if I wanted to come back home. I said, "No, Dad. I really want to stay here, and I am hoping one day I can leave this chaotic life and move somewhere with better opportunities and a better life." He started to lecture me as all fathers do to do something with my life. Since I was not coming back, he admonished me to try to get married and have a family. I told my dad I would do that but without conviction. He did not understand how hard that would be for a single man with no family at the refugee camp to find a girl and get married. At any rate, that was not my priority at all at that time. I needed to get out of Turkey and start a new life. Our emotional meeting came to a quick end, and I hugged them both again and told them I loved them and would hopefully see them again soon. That was the last time I ever saw my father.

A few months later, I received news that he had passed away. I sat in my tent with tears streaming down my face, cursing my stubborn pride and idiocy. I was a young fool and too determined, so I had not listened properly. Who could have known that our brief meeting at the fence would have been the last time I would see my father in this life? If I had known, I would have left at that moment and stayed with him as long as he was there. My dream felt so big in my mind that I could not see anything else. Now suddenly, I felt very selfish. I should have been there for him. I should have been there for my mother. I am not sure what difference I could have made other than being with him a little bit longer while he was alive, but I missed my father so much, and it felt like I had a deep empty well inside my chest where my heart had been. My dream was so distant and small, and I had sacrificed the few moments I could have spent with the greatest man I had ever known for something I didn't even know I would ever see.

Losing My Father

Losing my father led to a stupid daring action that almost stole my dream forever. It was midnight in the winter of 1992 when some of my colleagues and friends returned to the refugee camp to bring the very sad news. They told me my father had passed away many days ago. When I heard that news, I felt a heavy pain going through my body, and I could hardly breathe. The news hit me so badly. I did not know what to say or how to respond to my friends. I just started crying; tears poured out of my eyes. My tears were flowing down my cheeks, making my young mustache and beard wet. Of course, at the refugee camp, we did not have any kind of tissue, so I just used my old clothes to dry the tears on my face. I was amazed at how wet they became. That night, I could hardly sleep. It was hard to lose my father without any of my family members around me. My father was not only a father to me; he was my best friend and greatest mentor. The hardest part of this mourning was not being able to see him before his death. I was told he had a heart attack and, a week later, he passed away. I was thinking if I had known that, I could have seen him before he left me forever. So many things were going through my mind. Nonetheless, nothing mattered, because I was told he had been buried almost a couple of weeks ago.

The next day, all my friends around the refugee camp rallied around me. They came to my tent to offer their condolences, and it was some comfort to know others cared so much. Most of them were very supportive and offered their help whatever they could to comfort me. My good friend Fuad had seen my distress the night before and quietly asked me privately if I wanted to go home to see my family. I asked him how it would be possible. He reassured me and said, "Do not worry about how, but let me know if you want to go." He assured me that he would take care of everything. He knew I did not have any money or a connection with anyone to take me back to Kurdistan and then come back. He was so sincere, and I was in such grief that I obviously agreed with the idea, so he told me about his plan. He knew someone who could smuggle me through the border and cross the river on the Zakho town side; from there, we would go through Zakho and travel back to Erbil. The whole trip would only take a couple of days; Fuad had planned everything.

Fuad Ali, and Dr. Bewar

A few days later, I snuck out of my tent after midnight. It was very scary because our refugee camp had guard towers and was surrounded by Turkish soldiers. The wall had barbed wire similar to a concentration camp or prison. It was not an easy task to secretly leave the camp. If you left by the front gate, it was easy, but you could never come back. I wanted to come back, so I knew I had to take the dangerous route of escaping over the wall. As a matter of fact, one of my friends, Azad Hama Russel, was shot at the refugee camp, trying to sneak out, so I knew I could easily be shot by the guard, and no one would have said anything. Nevertheless, I climbed the wall of the refugee camp. I carefully avoided getting snagged on the barbed wire on top of the wall. Fuad was helping me, and then I jumped to the other side. Our refugee camp was situated on the main highway between Zakho-Kurdistan and Silopi-Turkey. Anyway, after getting to the other side of the fence, I had been told to walk toward the small village which was on the border close to the camp. There, I met the man who was supposed to take me to Zakho without charging me. I believe the smugglers were charging each individual about $200 to get them to the Iraqi Kurdistan. Most of them were smuggling cigarettes and loose tea to sell in Zakho. I remember how the smuggler skillfully crossed the river as we were walking behind him and following every step he was taking. I knew that someone had paid him well to take care of me. I thanked God for Fuad.

After arriving in Zakho, I stayed with Fuad's brother-in-law overnight, and the next day, I rode a taxi to Erbil. I will never forget Fuad and what he did for me. Along with the smuggling and directions, he gave me money—I'm not sure and do not remember how much—and gave me a pair of shoes, along with new Kurdish clothes. He took care of every need for me and undertook complete responsibility and made sure when I came back, the same guy would bring me back to the refugee camp.

When I arrived in Erbil, it was late evening. I went straight home. The moment I stepped into the house, my mother, brothers, and sisters all ran toward me. It was a very sad time for me. What was the saddest time for me was that it was the first time I ever walked into our house without my father being there. My older brother

Bakir came toward me and held me very tight and said, "I am so sorry, brother. I really miss my father too." I had never seen my older brother Bakir cry that hard before. That day, I was very happy to be with my family even though it was for a sad reason I had come back. Again, I had good food and a warmer bed, and I could take a hot shower. The next day, my family took me to the cemetery to visit my father's grave. I could not stop crying for hours. My mother told me, "Please stop. He is in a better place. He was a good man and a good Muslim." After a week of mourning and comforting one another, I decided that I needed to get back. If I stayed too long, I would lose my nerve and never see my vision. However, when I told my family I was planning to go back to Turkey, they all were against it, especially my older brother Bakir. I finally had to lie by convincing him to let me go because I had some personal belongings and I needed to get them. I'm not sure if he believed me or not, but he finally relented. I knew I did not want to come back to Iraq in this situation, so I had to come up with some reason to get them to let me return. I was determined to leave this world and never look back. The situation back then in Kurdistan was so bad. I was 100 percent sure, once I got back to the refugee camp, I was going to a country where I could build my life.

The next day, I got into a taxi and left—straight back to Zakho. When I arrived there, I stayed overnight at Sarkwat's house, which was Fuad's brother-in-law, and the next day at midnight, the smuggler took me back into the camp. It was a long journey, but I was ready to go back to my little cold tent. I felt that I had left my family sad and depressed, but at least they were safe. Just a few months later, however, troubling news hit me again. I received news of the tragic death of my older brother Bakir. My older brother had advised me not to go back to Turkey and to stay with our family. I had again blindly rejected his idea and did not listen to my older brother, just like I had not listened to my father.

Tragic Death of Bakir

My older brother did not die from natural causes like my father. Instead, he was killed by an unknown Iraqi intelligence assassin. That is all I was told by the people who related his passing. His death hit me even harder than losing my father. After the death of my father, Bakir replaced my father's role and took care of my family properly. He had his own family as well, but when he was murdered, he left a wife and four children behind. My brother was everything to our family: intelligent, business-minded, a Peshmerga hero, and highly respected in our community. By losing him, our family was devastated. To this day, we have not recovered fully from his loss. He had many strengths that promoted industry and success for us even while my father had been alive. It was he who had decided to start our family agricultural business. It was he who had changed our family fortune as well. My father had always shown tremendous respect for him because my brother had earned it from my father. Bakir had built family wealth, respect, and a family. Now his absence left a large hole in our family that was impossible to replace.

I grieved by myself for a while at the refugee camp. Yet again, I wanted to go back and visit my family. This time, however, I was able to get permission to leave the refugee camp legitimately (well, mostly legitimately). One of my colleagues told me that many people were going back to Kurdistan and the UN was taking care of their expenses. So he suggested buying a name from the UN list of individuals allowed back into Iraq. I believe it cost about fifteen or twenty dollars. With the fake name, I could travel through Mosul going through the Iraqi checkpoints without any issues until I arrived home in Erbil. So I quickly bought a name (I don't remember who the person was. I only had to use it when I went to the UN office and told them I wanted to go back to Iraq. I had to avoid calling my home, Kurdistan, as it was not allowed in the refugee camp or in Turkey in general). I soon found myself getting into a truck full of people who wanted to go back to Iraq and travel through the Iraqi checkpoints.

The UN took us through Mosul, which was a much shorter journey than traveling through the Kurdistan Regional Government (KRG)–controlled area. I was happy I did not have to travel for days to go back to Erbil. We left around 10:00 a.m. and crossed the Turkish border. When we arrived at the Fishkhabour, Kurdistan-Iraqi border, I went to the PUK office. There I talked with Mamosta Baker, with whom I had previously served as a Peshmerga under his command. He welcomed me back and then recounted what he knew about my brother's martyrdom. He offered his condolences and told me to let him know if he could be of any help.

After a very short period of time spent at the PUK office, I left Zakho and traveled through Mosul. We arrived in Erbil in the afternoon. My family did not know I was coming home, and I did not feel confident enough about my feelings to call them on the phone, so after we were dropped by the UN truck, I hailed a taxi, which took me straight to the Adallah area where our house was located. I got out of the taxi and sheepishly knocked on the door of our house. I wanted to be with them more than anything, but I also dreaded walking into my home again. I had left with the shadow of my father's death engulfing our family and even before that loss had lessened with the passing of time another dark shadow had fallen with the martyrdom of my brother.

The minute I entered our house, I was faced with such pain. It is hard to describe. Everyone was crying. My mother was especially devastated; she could not stop crying and singing for my brother with her broken voice. She was chanting a mourning song and, at the same time, reflected her memories of my brother with the nostalgic song. I went to each member one by one and held them. They were surprised to see me, but what should have been a joyful reunion was tainted with the despair of the situation.

While I stayed with my family, the hardest sight to witness was my niece and nephew, the daughter and son of Bakir, sitting in the corner of the house, crying for their father; it broke my heart to see their anguish, confusion, and anger. It was so hard to watch them that I almost wished for death to take me and us all to avoid witnessing such a horrific scene. My family was in such low morale. After staying with them for some time, I came to realize that I could not do anything for them. I was an outlaw in the country. I could not work, and I could not have a business. In fact, just staying with them puts them all at risk from the government or from warring factions in the Kurdish power structure. I knew that the only way I could help them was to return to Turkey and get to America. There I knew was where my destiny lay, and I would change my fortune and the fortune of our family. I went to my family and told them of my resolve to return to the refugee camp.

They were aghast. They asked me how I could even think about going back. They even threatened that they would disown me if I went back; they would forget my name, and I would be dead to them. Though it nearly killed me inside, I knew they were speaking from the pain and grief, and not thinking rationally about the future. If I didn't go soon, I would never be able to fulfill my dreams, and they would never get the help they needed. In any case, I had made up my mind, and I was stubborn as the mule I had beaten to death as a child. I decided to go, anyway. I did not have any money to travel with, but my good friend and cousin Aziz (who was later killed in 2014 during a fight against ISIS) knew about my situation. He offered to lend me some money so I could go back to Turkey. The couple hundred Iraqi dinars that I borrowed from him secured my destiny.

The next day, I quietly left my home without telling anyone I was going. As I quietly closed the front door, I was silently crying knowing I may never see them again, and even if I had another opportunity, they may never recognize me as their son and brother. I quickly went to the Garage Taxi station and left for Zakho. I was determined to leave Kurdistan. I knew there was nothing I could do even if I stayed with my family. Culturally and traditionally, I should have stayed with my family. The emotional drama of our family was very high. No matter what I would have said at that time, they would have never accepted my departure. As a result, I made my decision without thinking about the eventual fallout and left Kurdistan to go back to the refugee camp.

US Embassy and My Interview

Even though I had lost my father and brother while in the camp, I still came back to the refugee camp and wanted to leave the region. I know many people, including my own family, thought that I was very selfish. They told it to me directly so many times I could not shake it from my thoughts. I told myself over and over that I had to return to the refugee camp because it was the only place I could talk with the US embassy. Those remaining Kurds in the camp had already been passed over by all the other countries that were accepting refugees, and the US embassy was the last government that could accept us. If any of us was not approved and accepted by the US embassy to travel to the United States as a refugee to resettle, we were out of luck and would be forced to return back to Iraq. It was a crucial moment in my life and everybody else's as well. So I had to return to the camp to be present when the time came. I also was determined to do whatever I could to be selected. Every refugee knew that they had to do the impossible to be accepted. Whatever we had to do, lie, cheat, or make up a novel story, it did not matter; we had to make sure our story was bought by the US government to leave this tragic life.

After a year and a half, my name was finally selected by the UN to have an interview with the US embassy. For security reasons, the US embassy personnel did come to our refugee camp (I suspect it was due to the Turkish government's prejudice and lies they would tell the US government that the PKK armed resistance group would target them). Whether those were just rumors we spread in camp or if it really happened, they would, nevertheless, not come near our camp.

I remember the UN brought us a bus and took us straight to the Ghazi Antab, a city that was about a four-hour drive from our refugee camp. The excitement was there, along with the anxiety about my destiny. What would happen if the US government did not accept me! What could I do? I did not want to go back, no matter what happened to me. Maybe I would stay in Turkey or escape to Europe. I didn't want that. I wanted to start a new life with security and opportunity, but more than anything, I wanted to make sure I was not forced by the UN to return to Iraq.

When it was my turn at the US embassy-consulate, I gave my interview with the person in Gaziantep. I was very confident about my interview, which I kept thinking about all that night in Gaziantep. The next morning, I was sent back to the refugee camp to await their decision. That one night in a real city though was like a breath of fresh air. It was different and fun to see an actual city. I was like a prisoner when I stayed at the camp. Even when I traveled to my home in Erbil, I had not been free to move around and see the city. Going to such a big city gave me such a view of the possibilities. I felt like I was alive again. I imagined the day I could go back to civilization with real people living normal lives where I could start living my life again. The next day, when I went back to the Silopi refugee camp and started living in a tent again, I was more depressed than ever.

Refugee Status with the US Embassy

All governments move slowly. The bigger the government, the more bureaucracy they have to move through to get anything done. The UN is one of the largest bureaucracies in the world. When I was told I would have to wait for their answer, I knew it was not going to be a week or two or even a month. We had to wait for six or seven months in our desolate camp to get news from the UN about our interviews. It was unnerving not being able to check the status or get updates on where they were in the process of whether we had been accepted or denied entry to the United States of America as refugees. The time seemed to pass in a daze. It didn't go quickly per se, but it just seemed to float along like a boat on a calm river eventually will get to its destination. I was in the boat with no oars and completely at the mercy of the officials who controlled the current. It was maddening.

Finally, one day, we heard noises from the UN office in our camp. They were making an official announcement: "Attention! Attention! Please come to the UN office." The PA system boomed over the speakers throughout the camp. "We have received the names of those individuals and families who have been accepted to travel to the United States and resettle there as refugees." Everyone rushed to the UN office or huddled close to the speakers in hopes they would hear their name called.

This moment of my destiny had finally arrived! All my hopes, dreams, and ambitions were suddenly on the crackling voice emanating from the old speakers. It was so silent in the camp aside from the voice. We all were listening carefully, and no one dared to utter a word. Mothers and fathers were hushing their children, and the children themselves seemed to be holding their breath as though they understood the importance of hearing their names called. The UN official who was reading the names was a man I had met a few times. His name was Ismat. He was a Kurd from Turkey. He explained that he would start alphabetically by last name. I was happy about this since my last name started with *B*. I was with my friend, Shawn, listening to the announcement. He read through the *A* names and then worked through the *B* names. Suddenly, I realized he was on the *C* names. I had not heard him say my name! I started to panic inside but kept listening. Perhaps my name was out of order, or they had reversed my first and last names, which sometimes happens. He kept on going. I heard all of my friends' names, including Shawn, read correctly. He passed the *K* names, and I was feeling frantic inside. I was suddenly engulfed in the fear that I would be deported back to Iraq. Something heavy seemed to have been dropped on my chest; I could hardly breathe. Tears of fear and frustration welled up in my eyes, and I frantically fought to keep them in control. I was so nervous and heartbroken. I had given up my home, my family, everything for this dream, and now the voice was telling me that I had been rejected. I had failed. Shawn saw my distress and gave me encouragement. They probably just made a mistake and accidentally skipped reading your name, he said. "I am positive you are on the list that they posted. They just made a mistake." He took my arm and started walking me over to the posted notice of the refugees. "Come on, let's go check out the list. You know they will hang the list for sure by the UN's office."

From Right: Shwan Hamad and Dr. Bewar

As we walked toward the UN office, I saw the look of disappointment on the faces of my friends and acquaintances in camp. We listened for our own names, of course, but we also listed to those for whom we had come to know and respect in our circumstances. Seeing the pity on their faces only enforced the thought that I had not been included on the US list. My friend Shawn, however, never lost hope. He pulled me right up to a group of people looking at the list hanging on the notices board. I was so hopeless and depressed that I didn't even make an attempt to go near the list. I just let my friend Shawn read it. As he stared at the list and looked, he started yelling. "Bewar, you are included on the list!" He started jumping and laughing out loud. I could not believe the news or what he was saying. I thought he was pulling a cruel joke, but he pulled me to the and pointed to the *B* section, "Look here!" There was my name in all its humble glory, Kamal Bewar. My name *was* included! We start hugging each other and jumping up and down. He laughed. "I told you, you were on the list. I knew they must have passed over your name and forgot to read it." I didn't know what had happened then with the reading. It had been one of those terrible moments I had had too much of in my life. I had lost family and friends. I had been shot at and starved. I had gone through so much, but somehow having my dream ripped from me like that had been just as scary and devastating. Then to have it suddenly appear back in my hands seemed like an impossible gift.

Later on, my friend and I were talking about what would have happened if my name had not been included on that list. I know my whole life would have been different. Some of my friends had actually not been included in that list, and as a result, they had returned to Kurdistan or Iraq. The journey of their lives is totally different compared to my own life. Some of my friends, after going back to Kurdistan, became Peshmerga and were killed in the fighting. Others simply returned to the quiet life of second-class citizens. I am happy for the chance I was given but wish more of them could have come.

Dr. Bewar leaving Refugee Camp

A New Suit for America

Before I left, a good friend named Hendren, another single male who had been a teacher in Kurdistan, came to visit me in my tent. He was approved as a refugee through the IMO to take him to Norway. He came to talk with me before he left. He knew that I had no clothes and that I would be going to the United States. He took his nice black suit with a shirt and a beautiful black tie as well. He gave them to me saying that he wouldn't need them where he was going. At any rate, he had other clothes, and I had nothing. I was so humbled by that man's generosity. I was excited to go to America, but he was right; I only had the threadbare rags I had lived in for the last two years. He didn't think twice about his gift to me, but it is just one more debt that I carry with me as a memory of the potential men have for greatness.

Handreen Swar

When I left Silopi camp in the United States, for months, I did not have any contact with my family. Also, they were all mad at me and did not want to talk to me because I left. I had been completely cut off. My mother was the only one who still talked to me; no one else even acknowledged that I was a relative. That's why I had no clothes and no resources. I was a complete refugee now. I had no family, no government, no one who would recognize me from my home and culture. That suit was all I took with me to America. It took many years of work to get my family to come around, but I sent money whenever I could to them, and after a while, they accepted me and acknowledged that I had done the right thing for me and our family.

Chapter 8

New Home

Arriving in Salt Lake City, Utah

It was June 4, 1993, when I arrived in the United States of America. The feeling of getting out of Turkey was great. Living in the refugee camp under the Turkish government for over two years was almost as bad as being under Saddam's regime. They treated us as though we were not good enough to be part of Turkish society as refugees. Suddenly, we were in America—the land of opportunity, the land of freedom and acceptance. I know that sounds naïve, but flying into New York International Airport, I was so relieved to finally leave all the issues of my home country and my life as a refuge behind me and to discontinue the constant humiliations.

Dr. Bewar—The day of arrival to New York City international airport—JFK

When I arrived at New York City international airport, I had only the black suit, and I had been given one small bag to carry in my hand. It had a big IOM (International Organization for Migration) logo on it. I was in a group of six single men. The nylon bag I was carrying had all our papers in it. Such as my medical test results, my name, where we will be going to and my final destination. I remember people looking and staring at us strangely. Glancing around, I realized why. We looked different. It was as though we had signs on our bodies that said, "We have been away from the normal civilized world and normal civilized people. Please stare at us." The way we looked, talked, walked, and even our clothes were all clear indications that we were different. My suit was not too conspicuous, but one of our colleagues was wearing his traditional Kurdish clothing, which made him stand out considerably. I am sure very few people at the airport had ever seen such strange clothes. Satar, my colleague, had been encouraged by other Kurds before he left Turkey to wear traditional Kurdish clothes so that the minute he arrived in the United States, journalists and reporters would be amazed by such beautiful and rare traditional coverings. They told him that he would be famous and they would surround him and take pictures of him. However, we did not see any journalists, and nobody mentioned his clothing or asked to take his photo. People just stared awkwardly as we passed. I believe he was somewhat disappointed.

The other thing that must have caused us to stand out was that we all had huge bags with an IOM logo on them that gave additional visibility to others to notice us. I am sure that most people had no idea what it meant. Now that I think about it, they probably thought it was a company logo or something. But since this organization had been our lifeline and had encompassed our dreams for so long, we thought everyone knew about it and were expecting refugees like us. The logo to me seemed to shout to the world, "Hey everyone, look at me. I am a refugee and just arrived here. Please do not stare at me like that, and accept me as a member of your society!"

Minutes later, we saw an IOM officer. He motioned us over to a couple more IOM officers who were waiting for us, and they took us to complete our paperwork with the immigration office. We didn't get a chance to see New York but were ushered immediately to another flight to Denver, Colorado. We traded planes one more time and then arrived in Salt Lake City, Utah. Everything was so new to us. We seemed to be making mistakes constantly, and because of how we were always treated before, we were scared that we would do something that would get us in a lot of trouble. For example, one of the men (Fakheer) got up during the takeoff to try to have another person take his picture. He got up out of his seat right during takeoff and handed his camera to one of his friends to take his picture. He wanted to get a view of Denver while the plane was taking off, so he was trying to get close to the window of the plane. At that moment, the flight attendant started calling him in English, which we didn't really understand very well, but her tone was obvious. She must have been saying, "Sit down, please. You cannot get up while the plane is taking off." He looked so embarrassed, and it was such an awkward situation that I started laughing so hard that I almost peed my pants. Though it was funny, it also showed me how far we were away from home and how much we had to learn.

We arrived in Salt Lake City around 9:00 p.m. The case manager from the Tolstoy Foundation Refugee Center, which was sponsoring us (the name has now changed to the International Rescue Committee or IRC), met us and introduced himself in Arabic. His name was Omer. He was an Arab from Palestine. We were four refugees all from Kurdistan of Iraq and single. He took us to our apartment in North Salt Lake. He quickly showed us some of the stuff in the apartment. Most of which we had no idea how to use or what it was for. He told us there was food in the fridge for when we were hungry, and he gave us each some money. I am not sure how much money he gave us, but I believe it was about $10. It was all so new to me that the paper he gave me meant nothing.

That night, I lay on my back in the warm bed underneath an actual blanket. There was no artillery shelling outside, no air raid sirens, no shouting guards, no night patrol walking. The wind could not creep under the flap of a tent or through the threadbare sleeping bag. My belly was full from a hearty, warm meal that wasn't just old beans or whatever could be scrounged from the countryside. There were no creatures crawling around in the dark, waiting to bite or sting. There were no troops somewhere in the dark that could attack at any minute. I didn't have my AK-47, and I didn't need one. The thick layer of dirt and grime was scraped off my body and washed down a drain with hot, clean water. There would be no night duty, no midnight foraging, and the future stretched in front of me as an open road of possibilities instead of empty dead ends. For the first time in nearly ten years, I was completely safe and full of hope. I fell asleep with a broad smile on my face. I hadn't slept that well since the innocence of my childhood.

Epilogue

I wish I could say that the rest of my life has gone smoothly. Although it has been much safer and I have had wonderful growing experiences, there have been many trials since arriving in Salt Lake.

Learning English, learning the culture, finishing my education, finding work, and learning to live in a new world are all ongoing struggles. Finding love and companionship and starting a family have changed everything. My adventure has continued, albeit in a completely different atmosphere; life still continues to amaze me. I am so grateful for this beautiful dream that finally came true.

About the Author

Dr. Kamal Bewar (Dr. Bewar) was born in Kurdistan, Iraq, in a small village (Peerdawood) in the governorate city of Erbil (Hawler in Kurdish). He grew up in this small community village, but before his eighteenth birthday, he joined the Kurdish Freedom Fighters (Peshmerga) fighting against the previous Iraqi government (Saddam Hussain's regime). After the 1991 uprising in Kurdistan, Iraq, failed, he moved to the refugee camp in Turkey. In 1993, after spending a few years in harsh conditions in a refugee camp, he migrated to Salt Lake City, Utah, as a refugee.

The day he arrived in Utah, he realized that life was not as easy as he had imagined. In fact, making a decent living requires better education and hard work. He was optimistic that opportunities exist in America, and he decided what the future would look like for him. Working two jobs and attending school was everyday life for this new immigrant. Dr. Bewar started working as a dishwasher, a candy company worker, a patient transporter at the LDS hospital, and a case manager. He worked himself up to become a translator/advisor with the US Embassy in Iraq and an assistant professor working with the Department of Defense.

Since he was a little boy, he has loved to read history, poetry, and novels. He has written numerous poems over the years and published his collective poetry in the Kurdish language. This love of learning pushed him to continue to educate himself with a bachelor's, master's, and finally, a doctoral degree.

Dr. Bewar speaks Kurdish, Arabic, and a little Farsi. He is the founder and president of the Kurdish Community of Utah. For most of his life, he has been working in education. In his current position as a student success coordinator, he works closely with students to ensure their academic and professional dreams are realized. He is passionate about assisting others in building their educational and career goals, especially those who have traversed the refugee and immigrant paths.

Currently, Kamal lives in Salt Lake City, Utah, and is a student success coordinator and adjunct professor at Salt Lake Community College in Utah. He lives with his beloved wife and son and enjoys the people, nature, and freedom that he finds in his community.

Printed in the USA
CPSIA information can be obtained
at www.ICGtesting.com
LVHW051053090924
790324LV00001B/82

9 798889 436270